Learning in the
Later Years

PRINCIPLES OF EDUCATIONAL GERONTOLOGY

Learning in the Later Years

PRINCIPLES OF EDUCATIONAL GERONTOLOGY

Victor M. Agruso, Jr.

Department of Psychology
Drury College
Springfield, Missouri

ACADEMIC PRESS New York San Francisco London 1978
A Subsidiary of Harcourt Brace Jovanovich, Publishers

To Ramona, Stephanie, Victor III, Valerie, Natalie

ACADEMIC PRESS, INC.
111 Fifth Avenue, New York, New York 10003

United Kingdom Edition published by
ACADEMIC PRESS, INC. (LONDON) LTD.
24/28 Oval Road, London NW1 7DX

Library of Congress Cataloging in Publication Data

Agruso, Victor M
    Learning in the later years.

    (Educational psychology series)
    Includes bibliographies.
    1.   Education of the aged.   I.   Title.
LC5219.A37   374   78–3329
ISBN 0–12–045250–2

PRINTED IN THE UNITED STATES OF AMERICA

Contents

Preface

It has become increasingly clear that education is required throughout the cycle of life. The educational foundation of the early years is but one major variable in the protracted development of the individual, since, if one is to survive in an enormously complex environment, one must continue to learn new things, new ways to adapt to changing conditions. Therefore, to study the nature of age related changes and differences among age groups found in the teaching–learning process would seem appropriate for a variety of reasons, one of which is preparation for the later years.

Experimental research provides compelling evidence that the elderly, contrary to popular belief, make continuing contributions to society in general, which leads, in turn, to the betterment of the elderly themselves. Thus, it would behoove teachers, students, and authorities in all fields to reexamine the ambiguities regarding learning and achievement potential in the elderly.

The aim of this book is to provide the reader with an understanding of the empirical research reported in the gerontological literature and to illuminate the theories out of which experimentation emanates. To this end, I survey the experimental evidence related to learning, memory, and intelligence in the older learner, as well as applications thereof. This book is thus directed to professionals (teachers and researchers) in education and educational psychology, as well as to graduate students in these and related areas. For those who would educate (teach) the older adult and for those who would train future educational gerontologists, this book is equally pertinent. It would also readily lend itself as a resource for persons working in a wide range of capacities with the elderly in their settings.

I have defined the emerging field of educational gerontology, tracing its historical foundations in the social and behavioral sciences and describing the nature of its relationship to the subdisciplines within these sciences, on which it is dependent as a branch of gerontology concerned with learning in the later years, all of which attempts to satisfy the need for a concise book on educational gerontology.

Throughout the book I suggest researchable problems found in the present circumstances of the aged, in the belief that research generated from this perspective will yield truly creative findings. This book describes and also explains wherever possible the nature of the learning process for the older learner, with an emphasis on those aged 65 and over. Although I am somewhat concerned with the broader issues, such as the effects of education on adult behavior in general, I focus on specific problem areas such as *real* age related differences (and the *real* significance of differences) in learning potential, in performance variables, and in memory functions. I discuss the limitations of age related research and the distinction between "age differences" and "age changes," so that future research designs and analyses may produce results translatable into effective learning environments for older learners. The book discusses age related limitations and the role that modern educational technology can serve to compensate for them so that, ultimately, maximum achievement, however defined, may be realized among the age groups.

The organizational scheme of the volume has been determined by its emphasis on empirical research findings that cut across the fields of general experimental and developmental psychology and that are first reported and then interpreted within the context of modern S–R learning or recent cognitive frameworks, whichever seemed more definitive or otherwise substantive. I have placed my emphasis on such findings because my concern is not with the formulation of theories, the resolution of complex theoretical issues, or the broad theoretical implications of highly complicated learning and cognitive structures that may or may not be testable; rather, I am interested in prediction based upon experimental evidence. Such evidence suggests that learning environments that increase the probability that maximum potential will be realized by the elderly can be created (modified) for them. In short, the book treats those aspects of cognitive behavior that are amenable to experimental analysis concerning the effects of aging as such. The themes of environment, learning, and reinforcement are apparent, which of course provide for a frame of reference.

I do not purport to have exhausted the experimental studies in adult learning, memory, and cognition. Instead, I have been highly selective, restricting my treatment to those task and organismic variables that should be of particular interest to educational gerontology at this point in its evolution. The variables discussed have immediate importance, and the study of them should form the basis out of which principle at some point is related to practice.

I would like to express my appreciation to Allen Jack Edwards, who read and criticized the entire manuscript. I would also like to acknowledge the assistance of Judy Armstrong and of the Drury College Library staff, who suffered through my many demands and went beyond what is expected in order to provide me with varied resources that were indeed helpful. Special thanks is due to Rabindra Roy, my friend and colleague, whose encouragement and suggestions greatly helped me throughout the preparation of this work. Finally, I would like to express my thanks to Barbara Baugh, who typed the earlier, cryptic drafts of this manuscript, and to Wanda Allie, who typed the final draft.

1

Educational Gerontology

Since the publication of *Senescence, The Last Half of Life* (Hall, 1922), a plethora of research findings have been published in gerontological literature on age related changes and the nature of the aging process itself (Riegel, 1973). Although others, Cicero and Galton (1883) for example, had in the past been interested in age related variables and their effects on performance, it was G. Stanley Hall who first stimulated the modern, systematic study of aging as a subject matter for a wide variety of investigations within scientific disciplines such as biology, medicine, anthropology, sociology, and psychology, all of which contribute to gerontology, the science of aging.

The multidisciplinary approach to the study of aging is requisite to the development of a coherent, comprehensive model capable of generating research that produces real answers to defined questions; however, it has raised profound ambiguities as to the nature of aging and the research priorities suggested to examine that nature. And although this chapter will deal with two models of aging, the emphasis will be on the cognate aspect of gerontology as a field of study (academic discipline).

EMERGENCE OF A NEW FIELD

A modern analysis of human behavior as a function of a chronologically defined stage of life was initiated by G. S. Hall in the early 1900s. Until that time
investigations had centered on phenomena of childhood and adolescence, with
little attention being paid to the nature of old age. It is curious to note that "senescence" was held to begin at about age 40. Hall (1922) suggested that specific
feelings, cognitions, and physiological states were characteristic of senescence.
He further suggested that senescence be examined not necessarily as merely a
stage in the continuing development of an individual but as a distinct (independent) condition or period of life. Although instructive, Hall's use of introspective
methodology, literature reviews, and anecdotal records as bases for publication
falls short of the scientific rigor of modern radical and moderate behaviorism
with its experimental analysis of behavior and operationism. Terms like "senescence" (with its pejorative connotation and biological implications) and "maturity" have been replaced by "aging" and "aged."

Presumably, studies reported in the literature of Hall's time emphasized age
related changes of the early years because most investigators believed that one's
behavior stabilized after puberty. The central focus for psychological gerontology in the first part of the twentieth century was found in studying psychic states
of the aged (Munnichs, 1966), and at the same time a high percentage of the
work emanated from medical and biological research centers (Riegel, 1973).
With the advent of Watsonian behaviorism, accent shifted to the dynamics of
change. The fundamental issues then became not so much concerned with probabilities but with such questions as: What changes as a function of time and what
is the nature and course of the change? Is there, along with the psychological
variables of aging, a constant factor to be defined?

Walter Miles (1939), one of the first psychologists dealing with the process of
aging, suggested that, rather than merely describe, the problem for the psychologist is to define the positive and negative aspects of the aging phenomenon
through experimental analysis and collaboration with scientists of other related
disciplines. Miles himself recognized fully the biological–physiological decrements sustained by the aging individual over time but submitted that the effects
do not represent a constant in aging (although deterioration itself is predictable).
On the contrary, the direction and nature of the effects are a function of one's
experiences. If one had positive experiences, the nature of which had yet to be
defined, then one's behavior was more resistant to biological–physiological deterioration which, in a sort of reciprocal relationship, was also a function of
one's behavior.

Psychology of Aging

More recently, James E. Birren (1960, 1964) defined the scope of psychological gerontology as research on the individual "as a complex system, moving for-

ward in time to further differentiation [p. 22]." The subject matter includes capacities, emotion, and social behavior "as they differentiate in the adult with age [p. 10]." For Birren (1964) and Shock (1967) the task of the psychologist (gerontologist) is to discover the mechanisms, the manipulable variables of aging so that, consistent with the overall aim of science, we can predict and control.

Since World War II there has been an enormous increase in the number of articles appearing in the major journals that deal with aging; these include *Gerontologist, Geriatrics, Journal of Genetic Psychology,* and *Journal of Gerontology* (Riegel, 1973). Historically, the literature of gerontology has been dominated by the neurophysiological aspects of aging; however, there is a trend toward investigation of verbal and cognitive functions in the elderly, aspects of behavior which also change over time. One reason for this additional emphasis is that it has become evident that virtually all conditions in our sociocultural milieu have been changing concurrent with, and perhaps independently of, the apparently changing individual. Presumably, conditions and individuals are changing at qualitatively and quantitatively different rates. However, some scientists, Kastenbaum (1971) for example, suggest that it is conceivable that, although the organism has aged biologically (and has therefore changed), it has not otherwise changed significantly from the beginning of adult years. Rather, what has changed are the general cultural and particular individual environmental conditions, which then provide inputs to produce the related outputs.

Perhaps one selects (I suggest this fully aware of the extraordinary difficulties in defining the functional stimulus) a new environment when one reaches the appropriate chronological age partly because of cultural expectations related to that age and not necessarily or solely because of bioneurological deficits that have forced a change to more "accommodating" conditions. Consider the different consequences possible if environmental conditions, including continuing education, were held relatively constant throughout one's adult lifetime. Also, from a neurological standpoint, if blood pressure could be stabilized or held at some level less than high, could then the "constant factor" of aging (i.e., the slowing down of all psychomotor reactions) be neutralized?

Hypotheses suggested by these enormously complex questions obviously must be tested within several disciplines, which in fact characterizes the current research picture. The problem, however, is that the vast collection of facts at our disposal, although assembled using well-defined scientific paradigms, have not produced a coherent body of knowledge; nor have uniform aging processes been identified (Schaie, 1973). According to Riegel (1973), this condition is partly the result of scientists' reluctance (because researchers with different priorities have been locked into formal models) to recognize the interaction effects of social and political conditions on human development. Perhaps the time has come for scientists to shed their rigidities, despite the fact that different disciplines have different orientations, and direct their energies toward the production of a coherent blueprint for aging.

At any rate, as was previously mentioned, there is a strong current interest in cognitive and verbal learning processes and their interrelationships in the elderly, since learning relates to a constant educational environment. Experimental research provides compelling evidence that the aged have more than sufficient intellectual potential and do in fact profit from education (Baltes & Labouvie, 1973; Granick & Friedman, 1973; Woodruff & Walsh, 1975). Moreover, to the extent that intellectual activity comparable to earlier periods is maintained, there is no significant loss (and in many cases there are gains) in mental acuity and performance parameters. The converse is true also, in that disuse or less than normal use leads to performance decrements.

One suggestion implicit in these findings is that perhaps age differences are a function of one's past and present formative experiences rather than necessary concomitants of the aging process itself. Therefore, it would seem appropriate for agencies serving the aged to provide educational stimulation for the elderly in the belief that increased productivity in the elderly is a function of increased participation in those learning and educational experiences. The dynamic processes related to the necessary and sufficient conditions for learning in the elderly will be discussed in Chapter 2.

Educational Gerontology

In view of the fact that performance increments are consistently observed during the later years, the psychologist's primary task is to explain the nature of intellectual abilities as they differentiate with age. Just as with younger persons, it would behoove the behavioral scientist to delineate the conditions of intellectual development for the elderly so that compensation can be made for any deficit and individual differences and a situation can be established for maximum achievement in each group. The branch of gerontology designed to research hypotheses generated out of this frame of reference is educational gerontology, which has the additional function of providing the academic community and other appropriate agencies with data transformed into practical models. What I am suggesting is that this subject matter area could be the mechanism that links together the collection of facts referred to earlier so that, being consistent with a pragmatic orientation, the elderly (and the world community for that matter) can profit more from the research findings.

Educational gerontology grew out of psychogerontology, which emphasizes a broad range of psychological variables. The scope of the former is largely limited to cognitive, intellectual, and educative processes in the elderly; however, it is also closely associated with related disciplines having common objectives, such as gerontology and the social sciences. Educational psychology can be linked with formal education in the first half of life and educational gerontology to education in the last half of life. Education of the first half is highly structured and formalized, whereas that of the second half is currently being "created," that is, a curriculum for adults is now being formulated. (One of the instruments assisting in this monumental task is a new refereed international quarterly journal, *Educational Gerontology,* edited by D. Barry Lumsden and published by Hemisphere Publishing Corporation.)

CHRONOLOGICAL AGE AS A VARIABLE

It would far transcend the scope of this chapter to discuss the developmental psychology of aging in great detail, since we are primarily interested in learning and performance as a function of age itself, fully cognizant that variables of a developmental nature are potentially functional antecedents of behavior.

Lepley (1934) observed changes in the shape of serial position curves as a function of age, which indicates that serial learning order varies with the learner's age. Although children served as subjects in these early experiments, Lepley suggested that the gross factor of age must be considered in future studies of serial learning order (see Chapter 3).

Sampling

Indeed, utilizing sophisticated research designs, investigators have conducted extensive studies on the nature of age effects along the entire age range continuum; however, it becomes quite another matter when comparative analyses of group performance are made. The problem is illustrated pointedly by the sampling difficulties encountered at the beyond 60–65 age levels. One difficulty is that the principle of randomization is violated simply because a group of persons aged 65 or over is not representative (since it has not been drawn randomly). Consider this, too: Researchers do not have physical locations or agencies for the aged from which a random sample can be drawn, since if they go to organizations of senior citizens or to residential communities for the elderly they will find the socially independent, intellectually active, and energetic (i.e., those not representative of the population as a whole). On the other hand, homes for the aged are composed, to a significant extent, of the less active and somewhat unhealthy (who, unfortunately, have been subjects in studies out of which many of our notions of the aged have been derived). Needless to state, a biased sample increases error greatly, thus compounding the uncertainty of conclusions that occur even under random sample conditions.

Just like other researchers in human behavior, gerontological investigators face the problems encountered as a result of the utilization of volunteer subjects, whose effects on data from studies dealing with aging have received little attention. The literature indicates a relationship between age and volunteering that goes beyond gross age differences. Although the situation of the volunteer subject of any age raises important interpretive questions related to the assumptions of sampling, there are also effects from monetary incentives (secondary reward) on the adult volunteer, which will be discussed in detail as we proceed through the text.

Gribbin and Schaie (1976) conducted a study to determine if subjects who are offered money for participation in an experiment differ in personality and intelligence factors from those who are not offered compensation. The subjects involved in this study ranged in age from 20 to 88 and were divided into seven age-level groups separated into males and females, some of whom were promised payment for their participation, while the others were not informed of any incentive conditions. Each subject completed a variety of personality and intelligence tests. Results indicate that monetary incentive had a negligible effect on determining whether or not a subject would participate in an experimental study. Interesting, however, is the fact that women, regardless of incentive condition, tend to volunteer more often than men and that middle-aged persons volunteered more readily than either older or younger persons.

Gribbin and Schaie suggest that the presence of monetary reward does not change significantly the nature of the "sample either with regard to age, sex, or certain personality and cognitive variables [p. 468]." They further suggest that their findings should not be interpreted as an excuse for not paying participants but rather as evidence that incentive conditions should be used discriminately or as appropriate to a particular design (a suggestion that closely parallels that submitted in Chapter 2).

In addition, Baltes, Schaie, and Nardi (1971) suggest that one's longevity is related to one's intellectual and/or cognitive ability to the extent that the brighter tend to live longer. This condition creates another source of bias, as exemplified in their longitudinal study in which subjects (the willing survivors) were tested at a 7-year interval to determine age related changes. Thus in this instance the variance probabilities of age on cognitive processes are somewhat lower than would be the case in an otherwise representative sample. However, according to Zubin (1973), despite their biases and practice effects, their historical and follow up values make longitudinal studies the best approach to the study of aging.

Another kind of sampling bias is found in cross-sectional studies and other modified designs in which the performances of various age groups are compared to determine age differences. The difficulty is that it is enormously complicated to attempt to control and of questionable validity to try to correct the effects of differing educational, economic, experiential, medical, and cultural backgrounds among the groups. Thus, for example, results obtained from an unhealthy group are conceivably a function of disease, whereas results (changes, for example) found in a healthy group are more likely to be a function of the aging process itself. Then, too, there is the added problem of operationally defining "healthy."

Age as an Independent Variable

The final problematic aspect of age as a variable is the extent to which it is used as an independent variable because results emanating from that kind of usage can be interpreted as mainly descriptive. Although some investigators have questioned age as a relevant concept in the definition of development, they offer alternative approaches in the study of behavioral changes related to chronological age that presumably yield data out of which explanatory mechanisms are derived (Baer, 1970; Baltes & Goulet, 1971; Birren, 1970; Kastenbaum, 1968). Age would not necessarily be replaced; it simply would take a secondary role in research designs, possibly as a dependent variable.

Historically, in the literature of child and developmental psychology, age (i.e., time) served as the basis of the classification system for researchers. The importance of this approach is that age can serve as a focal point in relation to which certain behaviors are described as occurring in some sort of order for the first year, second year, etc., on through senium. Baer (1970) discusses this "age psychology" in which the ordering of varying behavior patterns is the target of the psychologist (i.e., "the period in any organism when age change orders behavior change [p. 239]"). Age becomes the organizing feature in the research design. Baer, however, does not utilize age as an independent variable. Instead, he uses environmental variation, which yields a certain control over behavior. Thus age in itself becomes irrelevant. According to Baer, in the study of the antecedents of change, mechanisms of learning such as reinforcement and discrimination are defined more precisely than the age variable. Baer considers development to be a sequence of learning experiences.

Baltes and Goulet (1971) have summarized the major problems met in utilizing chronological age in experimental studies of developmental change and age differences. According to these authors, chronological age is an organismic variable "which cannot be varied, replicated and arbitrarily assigned as one would expect from a good experimental variable [p. 151]." Second, the meaning of chronological age is nonpsychological and derives its "psychological" meaning from its assigned relationship to psychological attributes. Third, age is related to a "timed" sequence of experiential phenomena, and functions at points or intervals along the age continuum are merely descriptive, not explanatory. Thus some investigators do not construe time as a cause. Rather, experimentally oriented researchers view behavior as a function of Genetic Blueprint X Environmental Conditions over time. A specific variant from this frame of reference is the Age X Treatment interaction paradigm.

At this point we are not particularly interested in the theoretical implications of the age simulation and age manipulation strategies mentioned in Baltes and Goulet (1971) as alternative approaches to the study of the developmental processes through which explanations of age differences are realized. Suffice it to say that an age simulation strategy identifies the factors related to performance changes within age groups. For a detailed discussion, see their paper. For an example and further commentary, see the discussion of Kastenbaum, page 11 and Birren, page 14 of this chapter.

The educational gerontologist should direct attention to applications of the age manipulation strategy in educational intervention programs. For example, the operant model utilizes this kind of manipulation for modification of behavior in learning settings and under other conditions as well (Baer, 1970); explanation is of secondary importance when little attempt is made to fit results into a theory of change.

In any case, it is therefore mandatory that educational gerontologists are aware of the limitations to age related research and of the distinction between "age differences" and "age changes" so that their own research designs and analyses will produce results translatable into effective learning environments for older learners who bring with them complex conditioning histories, perhaps significantly different from earlier learning conditions.

MODELS OF AGING

All the behavior discussed in this book is inextricably related to the nervous system, which is a critical factor in aging, since it is through its integrative and regulatory functions that the organism adapts to a changing internal and external environment. Thus it would behoove the educational gerontologist to have a basic understanding of the bioneurological changes concomitant with aging. It is only by keeping in mind the physiological restraints imposed by these predictable and in some instances invariant changes that the gerontologist will design an environment within which the aged might function to maximum potential. I do not mean to imply that because detailed discussions of other models, such as life-span or analytic, are not presented at this time that they lack significance. On the contrary, I am simply presenting two approaches to the study of aging that, taken together, represent a relatively integrated point of view.

A Composite Theory of Aging

Jarvik and Cohen (1973) have conducted an exhaustive review of the literature relating to the biological changes associated with advancing age, individual differences in rates of physical and intellectual decline, and factors that accelerate or retard the aging process. They placed their emphasis on the relationship of these issues to intellectual functioning during the advanced years, which will be discussed at great length in later chapters. My objective in mentioning their work at this point is to draw attention to a consistent finding: "The most pronounced change is a slowing of behavior. The precise biological events underlying this are still obscure, . . . but may result from an accumulation of waste products or an inefficient repair system [Jarvik & Cohen, 1973, p. 256]." In short, they conclude that biological and behavioral factors undoubtedly interact; however, investigators have yet to articulate the profound ambiguities arising from this enormously complex relationship.

Although antedating the Jarvik and Cohen study, Curtis (1966) presents a hypothesis which still appears to be tenable. (Bear in mind that although the investigators emphasized different aspects of the aging process there is some common ground and overlap between the two works; that is, Curtis considers only the disease-oriented aspects of aging, whereas Jarvik and Cohen are concerned with degenerative diseases only insofar as they accelerate aging and are otherwise related to cognitive function. Both are concerned with dynamic processes.) Descriptive studies demonstrate that a wide variety of diseases are concomitant with advancing age to such an extent (not uniformly, however) that it is very difficult for investigators to separate them from the effects of advanced age itself. In light of this fact, many researchers suggest that disease accounts for a significant proportion of the changes which take place during the aging process. Among these investigators is Curtis (1966), who defined aging as "an increasing probability of contracting one of the degenerative diseases [p. 143]."

Developing this notion further, he submits a composite theory of aging as a tenable hypothesis capable of generating research characterized by substantive findings. This theory encompasses several others that have been advanced by various researchers but rejected by Curtis as inadequate and insufficient as independent theories. They are as follows:

Wear and Tear—No doubt the whole organism wears down simply through exposure to an environment over time, thereby causing aging. Curtis submits that it is invalid as a general concept and valid only as a specialized concept, based on researchers' failure to cause aging in mice by "severe and prolonged nonspecific stresses [p. 143]."

Rate of Living Theory—The idea that aging is a function of stress and activity levels has considerable support; however, that it is the cause of aging is somewhat questionable in light of compelling evidence that exercise prolongs life in the human.

Waste Product Theory—Lipofuscins certainly accumulate in cellular locations over time; however, there is doubt whether the buildup does more than just interfere somewhat with cellular function.

Collagen Theory—A significant portion of the body's protein is collagen, the chemical composition of which changes with time, probably thereby causing some of the symptoms of aging, such as skin wrinkles. However, Curtis submits that this concept has limited application.

Autoimmune Theory—According to Curtis, this should be classed as a degenerative disease and not a theory of aging.

Somatic Mutation Theory—If the chromosomes are damaged (through radiation, for example), they may "fail to synthesize an important protein [p. 144]." The damage (mutation) may "accumulate until a large percentage of the somatic cells of the body are functioning poorly [p. 144]," which likely leads to signs of aging. Curtis feels that this theory states a significant factor in aging but that the effects of mutation have been somewhat simplified by postulating, for example, a 40-year latency period from the production of a mutation and "its final expression as a tumor [p. 144]."

Thus Curtis submits his "composite theory," which takes into consideration all the aspects of the foregoing six hypotheses. (Again, it is beyond the scope of this book to go into a detailed explanation of such enormously complicated neurobiological theories.) At any rate, Curtis views aging as a multistep process in which each step represents a different form of cancer culminating in the final step—death. Stated differently, aging is a function of many different cellular contingencies and is not accounted for by a single biological mechanism. "The most striking single fact about aging is that the probability of occurrence of a degenerative disease is very low in young adulthood but rises steeply during middle life to become a virtual certainty in old age [Curtis, 1966, p. 148]."

Neural Aspects of Aging

The neurobiological literature indicates that all cells eventually die as a function of aging processes; however, our concern is mainly with age changes in the neurons (and necessarily in the neuroglial cells) of the central nervous system, since these cells, which do not divide, are involved in learning, memory, and the other intellectual processes that are at the core of this book. According to Bondareff (1977), the neuroglia increase with age. Since neurons are replaced by neuroglia cells when they die, the death of neurons would then be concomitant with aging (although the evidence appears to be somewhat equivocal). Bondareff (1959, 1977) also reports a consistent, age related decrease in brain weight and volume, and although the causes of these changes have not been clearly identified, it is conceivable that they are a function of degenerative disease or perhaps of normal aging itself. In addition, a decrement in cerebral blood flow, along with a concomitant decrease in oxygen consumption in neurons, has been consistently reported.

Despite the apparent invariance of reduced brain size with age, many researchers submit that neuronal loss involves specific parts of the brain rather than a general loss throughout the central nervous system. Brody (1955), for example, reports a greater loss in the superior temporal gyrus than in the post central gyrus, with varying losses in other regions of the brain, and the frontal cortex sustaining more loss than the cerebellum. The literature of aging, in short, reports a decline in quantity of neurons within cortical networks after about age 50; however, it should be emphasized that there are procedural limitations in the morphological techniques used to estimate neuronal populations (Bondareff, 1977).

The implications of these changes for synaptic transmission are highly speculative at this time; however, investigators do report decreases in acetylcholinesterase activity as well as decrements in serotonin, dopamine, and norepinephrine content in specific regions of rat and human brains, all of which can be interpreted as evidence for age related changes in neuronal functions.

Perhaps the foregoing changes are a function of a genetic blueprint or the inevitable effect of maturational processes. On the other hand, the changes could be largely a function of environmental factors subject to manipulation. In later sections I shall discuss some of the issues surrounding the notion that the neurological base for some intellectual functions shows a substantial decrement in the advanced years, thereby accounting for the variation in learning performance related to certain abilities.

Behavioral Model

As the table of contents indicates, this is a book about the effects of aging on behavioral constructs such as learning, memory, and intelligence. Behavioral gerontology is concerned with the description and explanation of behavior changes in these and other functions as the organism advances in age. Specifically, I will discuss the learning theory model, which posits that behavior changes concomitant with aging are a function of learning. In other words, behavior changes observed in the elderly are subject to the same principles and mechanisms of learning as any other behavior change at any given period.

Although operating from the developmental field perspective, Kastenbaum (1968) provides us with an instructive example of how one learns to "behave old." Assuming that behavioral slowness is a function of "the total transaction between an organism functioning at a particular developmental level and its particular momentary environment [Kastenbaum, 1968, p. 282]," consider this: A young adult is placed into a contrived environment in which events occur at a rate faster than usual for this individual, so that behavioral output is slower than the enviromental pace. This condition parallels that which is typical for the old person in relation to the environment. What we have is "a situation in which a chronologically young person is functionally aged with this one basic characteristic of oldness [p. 282]," that is, behavioral slowness. In addition, the young person modifies other aspects of his behavior by behaving less, which is also characteristic of the aged. Through behavior modification techniques this young person behaving old will learn strategies with which to adapt behavior to the "altered tempo balance between himself and his environment that may occur as he does reach the later years of life [p. 283]." The predicted outcome is that his behavior "is less likely to be 'too slow' [p. 283]." That is, the young person would learn the appropriate responses (behavior) that lead to adaptation to such environmental conditions. Kastenbaum then suggests a strategy for implementing his assumption and makes his point that we should avoid "attributing the apparent aging of behavior to intrinsic developmental changes, when, in fact, there are other personal and environmental factors involved which could be manipulated if correctly identified [p. 283]."

Learning theory (operant version) assumes that virtually all of our behavior is a function of external environmental contingencies (Skinner, 1938). All one need do to control (and predict) human behavior, regardless of physiological decline, is to manipulate environmental stimuli (antecedents). And, despite the enormous complexity of the environmental stimuli and the potential range of varied responses (consequences) related to them, behavior can be seen as a function of them. This assumption does not preclude the presence and interaction of internal, physiological stimuli and one's genetic background as precursors to behavior. The emphasis in explaining behavior is simply placed on learning (conditioning) and, of course, the reinforcement contingencies through which learning is determined to a great extent. If our behavior is under the control of environmental stimuli and behavior that is adaptive is reinforced, then it would seem appropriate to manipulate those stimuli so that one's condition is improved when one's behavior is "adaptive."

By way of summary, the operant model incorporates two major principles in its functional analysis of the human organism–environment interaction:

1. Virtually all behaviors at all age levels are learned and can therefore be "unlearned" through variable manipulation and/or training. Thus, operant researchers emphasize the plasticity of most behavior in contradistinction to those who underscore the irreversibility of a substantial number of "aged behaviors."
2. Behavior is a function of the Human Organism × Environment interaction; for example, learning performance is a function of internal factors such as motivation and ability in interaction with external environmental conditions such as stimulus deprivation.

Krasner and Ullman (1973) point out that the manner in which furniture is set up in a hospital or school determines the variety and the limits of behavior in that setting. For example, classroom chairs arranged in a circle suggest that all the occupants of those seats have equal potential input, whereas chairs arranged facing one direction—toward the teacher—suggest that the authority (and the one to whom those seated respond) greatly influences the nature of the input.

Relocation Effect

Further illustration of the impact of environment on behavior is derived from compelling statistical evidence that the institutionalized elderly die at rates considerably higher than what would prevail had they not been relocated (Blenkner, 1967). Researchers studying the nature of this "relocation effect" on survival suggest that, once relocated, there are infinite psychological and physical variables interacting in the aged's survival, but it is the fact of relocation that is invariably related to mortality rate. Another hypothesis put forward to account for these excessively high death rates, especially during the first 3 months after relocation, are that the medically infirm, either because of psychological or physical causes, are the persons admitted to institutions and therefore would predictably die earlier than the noninfirm elderly who remain in their individual circumstances.

However, other researchers point out that when these variables are controlled for, the death rates are still higher than they would be had the infirm remained in their home environments. Other hypotheses pivot on the nature of care administered by institutions, suggesting that it is not of the quality the elderly would experience in home environments.

The evidence for a relocation effect is strong; however, it is not definitive and, therefore, conclusions stemming from it should be taken with reservation. In light of this, Blenkner (1967) offers the testable hypothesis that personal care and home management help, if initiated, will decrease institutionalization death rates and increase elderly survival rates.

Schultz and Brenner (1977) suggest that further research on the relocation problem, which is plagued by conflicting evidence, should focus on the individual's response to the *stress* of relocation, which is defined as home to home, institution to institution, and home to institution. These observers hypothesized that one's response is a function of: (*a*) the extent to which the relocatee maintains real or perceived power to predict and control personal environmental conditions before, during and after relocation and (*b*) perceived differences between pre- and postenvironments in terms of the relocatee's perceived control over the total milieu. Expressed differently, one's response to the stress of relocation would be measured by an increase, decrease, or no change in one's predicted mortality, presumably as a function of one's perceived potential to control and predict the course of one's life.

These investigators suggest that as the extent of choice (whether it is real or not is a moot question) increases, the negative effects of stress decrease as in correspondence to the increased predictability of the new environment; conversely, the negative effects of stress increase as environmental controllability decreases.

There seems to be little doubt that some form of stress impinges upon all humans in varying degrees. The question is: As one grows older, do the effects become more pronounced due to reduced tolerance to novel or otherwise negative conditions? Briggs (1968) suggests that the study of stress should receive high priority in gerontological research.

The suppositions that relocation can be considered a major life change and that significant changes produce stress related to concomitant psychological and physiological reactions in an individual, who thereby becomes more susceptible to disease, have received considerable support (Dohrenwend & Dohrenwend, 1974; Kiritz & Moos, 1974).[1]

Thus what we have here is environment, contrived or by its very nature, acting as a powerful factor in determining the range of behaviors emitted in that environment. As Schwartz and Mensh (1974) so aptly put it, in light of the enormous effect of environment on the aged, "How can one define aging apart from the environmental context (which includes societal expectations) in which the event occurs [p.7]?" Specific behaviors related to learning, memory, and intelligence will be discussed at length in the appropriate chapters.

In sum, the learning theorist (behavioristic version) assumes that conditioning is the single most powerful explanatory factor of human behavior in all of psychology. Critics, on the other hand, suggest that there are profound ambiguities in human experience that defy explanation by a system that considers the behavior of an enormously complex human organism through relatively simple principles of learning. They maintain this position despite the fact that the simple principles of learning theory include conditional probability of response (behavior) assumptions and an enormously complicated set of conditions related to reinforcement schedules. In later chapters we will explain the extent to which one's behavior is a function of a reinforcement system; this approach promises to provide clues leading to the betterment of the aged (and of society as a whole).

FIELD OF RESEARCH

Birren (1970) has established a rationale, along with a design for its implementation, for an experimental psychology of aging, in which independent variables are manipulated in order to reproduce changes that characterize a given chronological age. Slowness of behavior or behaving less are two relatively consistent attributes of the aged, both of which could be worked into a contrived situation to produce what Birren has suggested (see also Kastenbaum, 1968, p. 282), that is, the manipulation of variables attributed as causes of the effects

---

[1] Some changes, such as moves from adversive conditions to more rewarding conditions, are observed to reduce stress.

concomitant with aging. (The results, however, might be more descriptive than explanatory because of the nature of psychological and biological factors, which are at times highly inferential.)

It would seem that the discipline of educational gerontology should work toward establishing a relationship with the field of general psychology, and the developmental psychology of aging in particular, similar to the one which exists between the latter and educational psychology (out of which educational gerontologists emerge). Methodologies should be similar in their empirical approach; however, content should be dissimilar, with minimal redundancy. In addition, there would seem to be more of an "applied" emphasis in educational gerontology.

Systematic Body of Knowledge

We have considered what it is that researchers in aging are investigating and the ends to which they are striving; however, there is some question as to the existence of a coherent body of knowledge out of which they can produce something substantive. To begin our discussion, a distinction should be made between programs of graduate and undergraduate studies in the psychology of aging or adult development that are designed to train "gerontologists" (some of whom will develop an interest in educational gerontology) and continuing education or community college programs designed to educate potential "bachelor level" service personnel, the public, and the aged themselves. They are, obviously, interrelated, since both use the former's systematic collection and reporting of facts potentially translatable into testable hypotheses; however, because the aged and those actively engaged in servicing their needs are more concerned with selecting from the existing body of knowledge whatever is necessary for adaptation (survival) in specific environments, those involved in the graduate and undergraduate degree programs must take into consideration the broad range of problems faced by an aging population.

Models of Education

Further distinctions must be made between life-span education, lifelong learning, and andragogy, each of which fits into the scheme of educational gerontology, which, of course, is dependent upon other disciplines for comprehensive input. Life-span education emphasizes a planned series of activities, a program occurring within a more or less formal context and related to a developed curriculum (Monk, 1977; Peterson, 1975); this implies interaction between and among teacher(s) and learner(s). Lifelong learning, similar to life-span education in the sense that they both assume continuing potential and some sort of organized programming, refers to the changes brought about throughout one's lifetime through a learning context, either formal or informal (Peterson, 1975). As we shall see later, learning is a function of a complicated set of interacting conditions not necessarily linked to a formal setting. Andragogy views the adult learner as progressing through a series of problem-solving situations for which guidance and direction is provided by a teacher or other aide (Ingalls, 1973). The andragogical process requires for its success a highly motivated individual interested in understanding personal deficiencies and willing to work within limitations. At the minimum, there is one significant goal, that of improving or developing an integrated self-concept (Meyer, 1977).

The preceding models of education describe conditions for change in the behavior of the aging organism. Each functions under the compelling evidence that the elderly can indeed profit from novel experience, and each has the purpose of articulating the conditions under which the adult learner can maximize potential through an increase in knowledge and a refinement of skills; this leads to a better quality of life for the culture as a whole. The research data generated using these models will be discussed in detail in later chapters both in terms of coherency and applicability.

The Profession

That we have available in our discipline a workable (virtually systematic) body of knowledge is evident from the number of gerontological psychology graduate programs, both established and emerging, at highly respected universities. These institutions produce gerontologists, some of whom will specialize in the educational dimension of the discipline, either as research scientists, professors, practitioners, or as combinations thereof. However, as Lumsden (1977) has pointed out, programs designed specifically for educational gerontology are virtually nonexistent.

Gerontology is a growing field, as is indicated by (*a*) the increasing numbers of full- and part-time personnel working within the profession, (*b*) the existence of the Gerontological Society, and (*c*) the enormous research effort out of which new data and findings are being published in several journals that deal with the aged. However, its workers, teachers, and researchers have such diverse backgrounds and skills that its status as a single, cohesive, independent professional unit is highly questionable (Cox, 1976); the researchers, as pointed out earlier, represent a wide range of academic disciplines with varying priorities and loyalties, and the service personnel are composed of nurses, specialized therapists, social workers, a range of other semiprofessionals and a variety of nonprofessional attendant-like staff workers. Finn and Carmichael (1974) suggest that gerontology will ultimately be defined by subdisciplines in the form of (*a*) paraprofessionals with minimal training, (*b*) semiprofessionals, and (*c*) highly trained professionals who will be responsible for research and development. In time there will be more than sufficient numbers of teachers and researchers in gerontology who clearly identify with the field, which by then will have well-defined guidelines and educational programs for students. All members of the field will share in a common identity, sorely lacking at present (according to Cox, 1976). Once this identity has been established, the field will take on the status of other respected academic disciplines.

In any event, that high-level interest in aging has been sustained is exemplified through the amount of funds made available for research. For example, the National Institute on Aging, which took a major initiative in this area, saw a budget increase to $30 million for fiscal year 1977 from $16 million in fiscal year 1975 (Butler & Spieth, 1977).

Current Conditions of the Aged

The emphasis throughout this book is on the present circumstances of the aged, in the belief that research generated from this perspective will yield truly creative findings. Although we are concerned mainly with the learning conditions of the aged, we are fully aware of the bewildering number of other factors, such as political, economic, and quasi-social, that partially account for the variance in adult behavior from which we infer learning and therefore change.

As indicated earlier, there is little question of the aged's ability to continue to learn and to profit from experience; however, a question does arise regarding their attitude toward actually attending classes in a life-span education program. March, Hooper, and Baum (1977) conducted a study to determine the interest level of a group of persons aged 62 and over toward lifelong learning. The authors point out that although there are some highly successful educational programs for the elderly, they may be "attractive to only a relatively small number of older adults [p. 165]." The investigators used a survey questionnaire, the results of which indicated that 68% were not interested in attending (free) university classes and that only 32% were interested (as demonstrated by answering "yes" or "maybe" on the form). In fact, only one subject enrolled in the university the following semester. Granick and Friedman (1973) point out that one's present interest in continuing education is positively correlated with one's prior level of education.

Respondents in this survey suggested that "living is learning," that education is "the purpose of living," and that, in an informal way, they "learn something new every day." The authors point out that despite an entirely favorable environment, including more than adequate transportation facilities, their subjects simply did not participate in the available educational programs. It would appear, then, that perhaps we should determine more precisely the needs of the elderly before we design educational programs to meet these needs, the nature of which are profoundly ambiguous. This particular approach does not preclude academe's intervention in changing the present less than positive attitude of the elderly toward themselves and the attitude of the public toward the aged. I am inclined to believe that, through environmental manipulation, a "need" to attend class or something else with a structure can be engineered (i.e., the intrinsic and extrinsic worth [reinforcement value] of learning could be demonstrated). Although some will object to the exercising of this type of control over persons, they may re-examine their conditioned ideals regarding the nature of freedom in our demo-cratic society (characterized as it is by technological determinism) if they com-prehend the enormous benefits accruing to society through such continued learning.

At any rate, the need or interest to attend structured programs could be es-tablished, to a point, by demonstrating on a large scale to the elderly (and others) that one's quality of life can be significantly increased through development and refinement of intellectual and manual skills. As Jacobsen (1977) suggests, parti-cipation in educational opportunities has several goals, "but the primary motiva-tors are enjoyment, self-discovery, and community service [p. 51]."

The Elderly

In 1975 the U.S. Bureau of Census reported that persons aged 65 or over numbered 22.4 million (U.S. Bureau of Census, 1976). The median age of the total population is presently rising and, considering the current low fertility rates in conjunction with increased longevity, one can suppose that the aged popula-tion will show steady increases in number and proportion. In 1975, the number of older females exceeded that of the aged male population as follows: The num-ber of males per 100 females was 79.4 for those aged 65–69, 73.3 for those aged 70–74, 64.7 for those aged 75–79, 56.9 for those aged 80–84, and 48.5 for those aged 85 and over (U.S. Census, 1976).

As to what accounts for these significant ratio differences, Myers and Soldo (1977) report that stress could be the explanatory mechanism, since the male has been exposed to higher levels of stress (the effects of which are related to mortality) through his role in a highly competitive culture. However, the effects resulting from the changing roles of women, who now participate to a greater extent in one time male-dominated activities, could conceivably alter these sta-tistical trends. These observers also state that the chronic and degenerative dis-eases found in the later years tend to affect the male more often than the female, which, apparently, is partially related to the fact that women avail themselves of medical services more often and on a more consistent basis than do men.

Blenkner (1977) suggests several of the normal dependencies of old age, some of which are (a) economic, since one is no longer a productive wage earner and is therefore in a position of dependence on a variety of other, relatively uncontrol-lable sources of income; (b) physical, because of a decline in the efficiency of autonomic and central nervous system functions which initiates a condition of relative reliance on others for assistance or special considerations, which in turn affects one's mobility; and (c) social, in light of the loss of friends and of the roles through which status and other forms of reinforcement were once derived, so that one's general welfare becomes contingent upon the prevailing "social conscience."

In order to adapt these contingencies of aging, older persons will modify their behavior through self-imposed restrictions on personal and social activities, seek help from close friends and relatives in resolving common domestic problems, and participate in a variety of programs funded by government agencies for the aged and designed to compensate for their limited resources.

A major concern of the elderly is the fear of death and dying, phenomena that pervade their existence (Kastenbaum, 1969). However, this fear can be construed as a learned reaction, susceptible to modification through the application of learning (education) principles.

An increase in leisure time, brought about through the technological advances that have reduced both working hours and working years and through longer lifetimes, marks another dimension of the elderly's present situation. Insofar as one has the economic and psychological resources, leisure time can result in periods of happiness in which long-standing needs for self-realization are satisfied. Unfortunately, the majority of the current aged population are maintaining minimum subsistence levels (i.e., have marginally adequate incomes), and one in five lives in a condition of poverty. The older population remain in the inner cities or in small towns rather than move to suburban areas along with the more mobile, younger persons, all of whom are exposed to the effects of an industrialized society, albeit at differential rates. The elderly spend more time watching television and engaging in non-strenuous, solitary activities than the younger generation does. Leisure time is also characterized by long periods of relative idleness and reflection.

Approximately half of the current elderly population have not had a formal high school education; however, a significant number of those who will retire within the next 10–15 years will have had at least high school training, and it will be of better quality than that of the present older generation. Also, each generation from that point on will presumably be somewhat better educated and better trained than the preceding one.

Summary and Final Comment

It has become increasingly clear that there is no fixed description of an elderly population, since evidence demonstrates that each generation of older persons varies distinctly from preceding generations, not only in terms of numbers, but also in terms of type (Kastenbaum, 1971). For example, many of the present generation are foreign born or children of first generation immigrants, not fully acculturated, lacking in formal education, and whose main thrusts in life have been directed toward work, family, and religion. However, the emerging generation of the elderly, who comprise approximately 15% of the total population, are characterized by some of the more salient effects of affluence, such as relative financial security, substantial educational background which includes preparation for the retirement years, political clout, and, most importantly, a growing awareness that they are indeed contributing members of society who have worth for many reasons, one of which is that they have survived a rigorous selection process.[2]

The conditions under which they function are characterized by revolutions in technology, such as the medical advances that increase longevity; rapid social changes, such as the women's liberation movement; changes in professional-vocational patterns, such as the switching of careers in mid-life or later, and fewer working hours; changing value systems regarding the role of the nuclear family and of formalized religion; and, finally, the changing role of higher education in their lives, such as the increased opportunities to study, along with the diversity of such course offerings.

REFERENCES

BAER, D. M. An age irrelevant concept of development. *Merrill/Palmer Quarterly,* 1970, *16,* 239–245.

BALTES, P. B., & GOULET, L. R. Exploration of developmental variables by manipulation and simulation of age differences in behavior. *Human Development,* 1971, *14,* 149–170.

BALTES, P. B., SCHAIE, K. W., & NARDI, A. H. Age and experimental mortality in a seven year longitudinal study of cognitive behavior. *Developmental Psychology,* 1971, *5,* 18–26.

BALTES, P. B., & LABOUVIE, G. Adult development of intellectual performance: Description, explanation, modification. In C. Eisdorfer & M. P. Lawton (Eds.), *The psychology of adult development and aging.* Washington, D.C.: American Psychological Association, 1973.

BIRREN, J. E. *The psychology of aging.* Englewood Cliffs, New Jersey: Prentice-Hall, 1964.

BIRREN, J. E., Toward an experimental psychology of aging. *American Psychologist,* 1970, *25,* 124–135.

BIRREN, J. E. (Ed.). *Handbook of aging and the individual, psychological, and biological aspects.* Chicago: University of Chicago Press, 1960.

BLENKNER, M. Environmental change and the aging individual. *The Gerontologist,* 1967, *7,* 101–105.

BLENKNER, M. The normal dependencies of aging. In R. A. Kalish (Ed.), *The later years: Social application of gerontology.* California: Brooks Cole, 1977.

BONDAREFF, W. Morphology of the aging nervous system. In J. E. Birren (Ed.), *Handbook of aging and the individual.* Chicago: University of Chicago Press, 1959.

---

[2]The Bureau of the Census has reported in *Projections of the Population of the United States, 1977 to 2050, Series P. 25, No. 704,* that the number of persons aged 65 and over will be about 32 million by the year 2000. By 2050 the average life-span of females is expected to be 81 years and of males 72 years.

BONDAREFF, W. The neural basis of aging. In J. E. Birren & K. W. Schaie (Eds.), *Handbook of the psychology of aging.* New York: Van Nostrand Reinhold, 1977.

BRIGGS, J. E. Ecology as gerontology. *The Gerontologist,* 1968, *8,* 78–79.

BRODY, H. Organization of the cerebral cortex, III: A study of aging in the human cerebral cortex. *Journal of Comparative Neurology,* 1955, *102,* 511–556.

BUTLER, R. N., & SPIETH, W. Trends in training in research gerontology. *Educational Gerontology,* 1977, *2,* 111–113.

COX, H. The professional status of gerontology. *The Gerontologist,* 1976, *16,* 453–454.

CURTIS, H. J. A composite theory of aging. *The Gerontologist,* 1966, *6,* 143–149.

DOHRENWEND, B. S., & DOHRENWEND, B. P. *Stressful life events: Their nature and effects.* New York: Wiley, 1974.

FINN, M. W., & CARMICHAEL, P. Introducing pre-professionals to gerontology. *The Gerontologist,* 1974, *14,* 476–478.

GRANICK, S., & FRIEDMAN, A. S. Educational experiences and the maintenance of intellectual functioning by the aged: An overview. In L. E. Jarvik, C. Eisdorfer, & J. E. Blum (Eds.), *Intellectual functioning in adults.* New York: Springer, 1973.

GRIBBIN, K., & SCHAIE, K. W. Monetary incentive, age, and cognition. *Experimental Aging Research,* 1976, *2,* 461–468.

HALL, G. S. *Senescence, The last half of life.* New York: Appleton, 1922.

INGALLS, J. D. *A trainer's guide to andragogy.* (Rev. ed.) Waltham, Mass.: Data Education, Inc., 1973.

JACOBSEN, M. D. The later years: A season for continued growth. *Educational Gerontology: An International Quarterly,* 1977, *2,* 51–57.

JARVIK, L. F., & COHEN, D. A biobehavioral approach to intellectual changes with aging. In C. Eisdorfer & M. P. Lawton (Eds.), *The psychology of adult development and aging.* Washington, D.C.: American Psychological Association, 1973.

KASTENBAUM, R. Perspectives on the development and modification of behavior in the aged: A developmental field perspective. *Proceedings of the 76th Annual Convention of The APA.* San Francisco, California, 8-30-68.

KASTENBAUM, R. Death and bereavement in later life. In A. H. Kutscher (Ed.), *Death and bereavement.* Springfield, Illinois: Charles C. Thomas, 1969.

KASTENBAUM, R. What happens to the man who is inside the aging body? An inquiry into the developmental psychology of later life. In F. G. Scott & R. M. Brewer (Eds.), *Perspectives in aging II: Operational focus.* Oregon: Oregon Center for Gerontology, 1971, 37–45.

KIRITZ, S., & MOOS, R. H. Physiological effects of social environments. *Psychosomatic Medicine,* 1974, *36,* 96–114.

KRASNER, L., & ULLMAN, L. P. *Behavior influence and personality: The social matrix of human action.* New York: Holt Rinehart Winston, 1973.

LEPLEY, W. M. Serial reactions considered as conditioned reactions. *Psychological Monographs,* 1934, *46–56* (whole no. 205).

LUMSDEN, D. B. Graduate training in education and aging: Results of a national survey, Part I. *Educational Gerontology: An International Quarterly,* 1977, *2,* 429–434.

MARCH, G. B., HOOPER, J. D., & BAUM, J. Lifespan education and the older adult: Living is learning. *Educational Gerontology: An International Quarterly,* 1977, *2,* 163–172.

MEYER, S. L. Andragogy and the aging adult learner. *Educational Gerontology: An International Quarterly,* 1977, *2,* 115–122.

MILES, W. R. Psychological aspects of aging. In E. V. Cowdry (Ed.), *Problems of aging.* Baltimore: Williams and Wilkins, 1939. Pp. 535–571.

MONK, A. Education and the rural aged. *Educational Gerontology: An International Quarterly,* 1977, *2,* 147–156.

MUNNICHS, J. M. A. A short history of psychogerontology. *Human Development,* 1966, *9,* 230–245.

MYERS, G. C., & SOLDO, B. J. Older Americans: Who are they? In R. A. Kalish (Ed.), *The later years: Social applications of gerontolgy.* California: Brooks Cole, 1977.

PETERSON, D. A. Lifespan education and gerontology. *The Gerontologist,* 1975, *15,* 436–441.

RIEGEL, K. F. On the history of psychological gerontology. In C. Eisdorfer & M. P. Lawton (Eds.), *The psychology of adult development and aging.* Washington, D.C.: American Psychological Association, 1973.

SCHAIE, K. W. Developmental processes and aging. In C. Eisdorfer & M. P. Lawton (Eds.), *The psychology of adult development and aging.* Washington, D.C.: American Psychological Association, 1973.

SCHULZ, R., & BRENNER, G. Relocation of the aged: A review and theoretical analysis. *Journal of Gerontology,* 1977, *32,* 323–333.

SCHWARTZ, A. N., & MENSH, I. N. *Professional obligations and approaches to the aged.* Springfield, Illinois: Charles C. Thomas, 1974.

SHOCK, N. W. Current trends in research on the physiological aspects of aging. *Journal of the American Geriatrics Society,* 1967, *15* (11), 995–999.

SKINNER, B. F. *The behavior of organisms: An experimental approach.* New York: Appleton, 1938.

U.S. BUREAU OF CENSUS. *Current Population Reports. Series P-23, No. 59.* Demographic aspects of aging and the older population in the United States. Washington, D.C.: U.S. Government Printing Office, May, 1976.

WOODRUFF, D. S., & WALSH, D. A. Research in adult learning: The individual. *The Gerontologist,* 1975, *15,* 424–430.

ZUBIN, J. Foundations of gerontology: History, training, and methodology. In C. Eisdorfer & M. P. Lawton (Eds.), *The psychology of adult development and aging.* Washington, D.C.: American Psychological Association, 1973.

2

Learning

Undoubtedly, the common denominator observed among people is that virtually all of their behavior is learned or is otherwise influenced by experience. The interaction between experience and genetic background produces idiosyncratic behavior patterns for an individual and, indeed, for an entire culture. Given the pervasive effects of learning, it seems highly improbable that one can understand human behavior without having first grasped the fundamental principles of learning.

There has been an enormous amount of research on the psychology of human learning since the time of Ebbinghaus in 1885, and investigators in general seem to be approaching a unified position on the conditions of learning but not on the process itself, since, for one reason, the latter phenomenon is of a highly inferential nature. The trend toward a unified position is coming about through a gradual amalgamation of research findings from the traditional stimulus–response, associationistic paradigms with those of the more recent information processing, cognitive models. In addition, compelling evidence from research on the neurobiological aspects of learning and memory has given researchers a broader base from which to draw explanatory mechanisms.

Although the field of learning and memory is still somewhat lacking in coherency (i.e., the general theories are subject to question), our concern is not with formulation of theory but rather with prediction based on empirical research, in the belief that learning environments which increase the probability that maximum potential will be realized can be created for the elderly.

The present chapter will discuss the more recent experimental studies in adult learning that include but go beyond description to provide explanations of learning phenomena in the aged. Specifically, our major concern is with age related changes and the capacity to learn, since if one is to survive in an enormously complex environment, one must continue to learn new things, new ways to adapt to changing conditions.

DEFINITION OF LEARNING

The term "learning" refers to changes in cognition that may affect behavior and through it one's adaptation to an environment characterized by more or less diverse contingencies of survival. Obviously, one enters the world as a biological system defined by specific fixed functions. (The extent to which one is or becomes more than that is of basic interest to philosophy but of interest to psychology only insofar as processes and phenomena related to one's state are empirically verifiable.) For example, one is born with a central nervous system (CNS) containing a full complement of 10–12 billion neurons. Over a lifetime, these cells may or may not be utilized to their full potential, depending to a considerable degree on the nature of the neurobiological and environmental conditions in and out of which the individual operates. Thus, at any given time one can be viewed as a complex of behaviors shaped by an environment. Native anatomical equipment makes possible the entire process of human communication that occurs in uniquely defined contingencies of adaptation; that is, people learn to use a wide range of skills according to their circumstances. As Kimble (1961) states:

> Changes of behavior of the sort we call learning range from the simplest modifications of the simplest organisms, to the most impressive contributions of human intelligence. Learning is basic to the development of athletic prowess, of tastes in food and dress, and of the appreciation of art and music. It contributes . . . pathological maladjustment. It produces . . . the bigot and the patriot . . . In short, it influences our lives at every turn, accounting in part for the best and the worst in each of us [p. 10].

It is clear that Kimble considers learning to be a change in an organism's behavioral repertoire that can be operationally defined as a relatively permanent change in behavior brought about by experience or practice. This definition is generally acceptable to psychologists studying learning; however, there are some difficulties present in it. For example, what distinguishes learning from other factors that influence bahavior, such as fatigue, motivation, aging, or maturation?

"Relatively permanent" is used (and is admittedly inadequate) because, at this juncture, we are uncertain of the extent to which the effects of experience are lasting. In other words, the question of the permanency of experience is unresolved, as suggested in James's (1890, p. 127) question relating to whether or not the organism stores all experiences. It is evident, of course, that humans as well as species lower on the phylogenetic scale forget what has been acquired, despite the fact that the CNS changes as a function of learning (changes in such a way as to influence further learning). One could assume, however, that stored knowledge (what has been learned) is merely temporarily lost to retrieval because of interference effects or other intervening variables and that, under appropriate stimulus conditions, that "lost" information can be elicited, as is observed in performance.

On the other hand, to speak of "stored experience" could be redundant, thereby creating unnecessary ambiguities, since it would appear sufficient to speak of learning simply as a phenomenon involving CNS changes influencing observed behavior; that is, nervous system structures are presumed to have been changed substantially because of what has been learned and, to the extent that the organism's behavior warrants it, one can assume that learning (and therefore permanent change) has occurred within the organism.

The phrase "relatively permanent" is also used to recognize the fact that the central nervous system deteriorates as the organism advances in years. Loss of brain weight and a reduction in the number of cells is concomitant with this process of deterioration. Since once neurons die or are otherwise destroyed they presumably do not regenerate, there is the possibility that both potential and some stored knowledge is lost. (These latter points will be discussed at length in Chapter 3.)

Our definition includes the word practice, which distinguishes learning from those relatively permanent changes in behavior due to maturation (changes as a function of biological growth processes), injury, or disease. The definition of conditions of practice is also somewhat unclear but is generally taken to mean that the organism is operating on an environment.

According to Kling (1972), the term "conditions of practice" implies controlled exposure to specific experiences. He adds that: "Not all behavior that takes place under controlled conditions qualifies as practice; a defining characteristic is presentation of knowledge of results, feedback of information, or presentation of reinforcing or punishing stimuli [p. 553]."

He extends the definition of practice to incorporate classical conditioning,

which includes the presentation, in temporal orders, of conditioned and unconditioned stimuli. Practice would seem to be a necessary condition for learning to
occur, but not a sufficient one since, among other things, it produces fatigue
(inhibition and subsequent decrease in behavior). Some psychologists therefore
suggest that learning is a function of reinforced practice.

Learning versus Performance

The final distinction in our definition is between learning and performance.
Learning (a process) is always inferred from performance (an act), but to use the
terms interchangeably would create deep ambiguities (Hilgard & Bower, 1975).

The performance condition is temporary, since, among other reasons, its activity is restricted to a particular acquisition or retention task. As indicated earlier, one does not observe learning directly but instead makes an inference that
learning has occurred within the organism when the organism is observed as having been changed. That change has occurred is indicated by the actual behavior
performed; that is, a behavioral potential has been realized by the organism.

In sum, learning represents an underlying process which is but one of the
many determinants of performance. Expressed differently, performance is learning expressed in overt behavior that is also a function of state variables such as
set, motivation, fatigue, or illness. Performance is the objective measure or index
of learning; however, failure in performance does not necessarily mean that
learning is absent or has been forgotten, since performance is inextricably related
to other state variables.

A series of latent learning studies conducted by Tolman and Honzik (1930)
have established that such a distinction is tenable. In one study, rats deprived of
food and water were placed in a 14-unit multiple T maze daily for 17 consecutive days. One group was rewarded each day upon reaching the goal box, since it
contained food. A second group received no food reward. A third group received
the food reward only after completion of ten trials, that is, from the eleventh
trial to the seventeenth this group was rewarded with food. Examination of error
scores shows that the consistently rewarded group outperformed the no reward
group as well as the eleventh trial rewarded group until its reward was introduced, at which time their respective performance rates matched.

These findings, which have been replicated many times, provide strong support for those who make a distinction between learning and performance, since
the eleventh trial group's latent learning did not manifest itself in performance
until after the reward was introduced; that is, the rats learned about the alley
maze despite no reward, though the learning was not reflected in their performance during the first ten trials. Therefore, these studies strongly suggest that reinforcement (reward) is not a necessary condition for learning per se.

CONDITIONING

"Learning" is a term that is defined through a variety of procedures ranging from the analysis of the simple conditioned reflex (considered by some as the prototype for complex learning) to complex verbal learning. Studies generated under the rubric of conditioning provide descriptive and explanatory evidence along with prescriptive mechanisms for such problem areas in aging as the marked decrease in speed of response, the interference phenomenon as an increasing function of age, and the difficulty in forming new associations through either classical conditioning or other procedures. It is to experimental studies investigating the dynamic processes and environmental conditions related to these phenomena that we now turn.

Classical Conditioning

Braun and Geiselhart (1959) conducted a study in which they conditioned and extinguished the eyeblink reflex in three groups of male subjects divided into age groups of 8–10, 18–25, and 62–84 years. The conditioned stimulus (CS) was an increase in illumination on a small disk in front of the subject. The unconditioned stimulus (UCS) was a puff of air to the eye. The experimenters compared performance of each subject over 80 conditioning trials and 20 extinction trials. These comparison data indicate that the older group differed significantly from both the young adults and the children in terms of the total number of conditioned responses (CRs) over 80 trials; that is, the percentage of CRs was higher for both children and young adults. Resistance to extinction correlated positively with conditioning rates. The significant finding is the relative difficulty the older subjects had in the acquisition of the conditioned eyeblink response. It was noted that 4 of the 13 subjects in the older group gave no CRs during the 80 trials and 7 gave from one to eight CRs. The authors suggest that over many years the eyeblink response had been adapted out and was therefore less susceptible to modification by conditioning procedures. Although the investigators did not elaborate on the implications of the relatively high conditioning rates and longer response latencies of the children, Botwinick (1970) suggests that a neural responsivity problem might have been present.

Kimble and Pennypacker (1963) conducted an eyelid conditioning experiment over 60 trials in which 39 male subjects were divided into two groups of 18 young (mean age 20) and 21 old (mean age 67). Although the aged in this study gave more CRs than those in Braun and Geiselhart (1959), the results supported the findings of the earlier investigators; that is, older subjects did not condition as well as younger subjects. Presumably, the reason for the differences found in level of conditioning is that in the Kimble study the USC duration was

50, whereas in the other the duration was 500 msec. Apparently, the longer duration leads to more habituation of the UCR. Kimble and Pennypacker suggested that their relatively poor conditioning is a function of the elderly's marked habituation of the unconditioned response during the experiment.

Habituation

In view of the importance attributed to habituation in the Kimble and Pennypacker study, perhaps some further explanation of it is warranted. Although the reasons are unclear, it has been observed across species that an organism learns not to respond, at least overtly, to a stimulus event to which it has been exposed repeatedly. This phenomenon, which is considered by some (Kling, 1972, p. 592; Razran, 1971) to be a simple (only one stimulus as compared to CS and UCS in conditioning) form of learning, is referred to as *habituation*. In habituation, a response decrement to a particular stimulus is observed when that stimulus is repeated. For example, initially the sound of a train passing by one's bedroom during the middle of the sleep cycle is arousing; however, upon repeated stimulation of the sensory system by the train's noise, the noise no longer evokes a response. The individual has been habituated to it and no longer attends to that specific stimulus event; therefore, a response decrement is observed.

It has been observed that repeated stimulation can also lead to a response increment, as in the case of *sensitization* defined by Razran (1971) as a "more or less permanent increment in an innate reaction upon repeated stimulation [p. 58]." Unlike habituation, however, the response increment is not stimulus specific.

Finally, habituation must also be distinguished from other behavioral changes in which there is a decrease in responsiveness with repeated stimulation, such as *fatigue* and *adaptation*. Under conditions of *fatigue*, response decrement to all stimulus events is observed. When an organism's sensory apparatus *adapts* to an environmental stimulus pattern, the adaptation is to a broad category of stimuli; that is, one's entire visual system is sensitive to all stimuli, as in the case of the process of adaptation to darkness.

Operant conditioning

Unfortunately, the basic data on aging in research in the operant area is sparse; however, research coming from the operant model represents a significant contribution to our understanding of the ontogeny of intelligent behavior and of the nature of intervention strategies, which will be discussed later. Baltes and Goulet (1970) report that performance decrements in the aged can be improved using operant procedures. We mention the operant model in this context, since studies that explain functional relationships between reinforcement and learning in the elderly are needed.

Ayllon and Azrin (1965) conducted a series of six experiments in which a wide range of behaviors of psychotic patients were reinforced with many kinds of reinforcers in an attempt to increase desired behaviors (not to cure psychoses). It has been observed that the psychotic is characterized by an apparent absence of effective reinforcers. One approach in identifying potential reinforcers is to observe peoples' behavior during leisure hours. Once repetitive behaviors have been determined, they can be used as reinforcers according to the Premack principle (1959); that is, a high-frequency behavior can be used as a reinforcer.

The "prepotent response" theory of Premack assumes that any response has the potential to be reinforcing. The power of any given response is a function of its strength in relation to other responses, so that a stronger response can reinforce a weaker one. Response strength, in other words, is determined by the amount of time an organism spends performing an activity under conditions when two or more potential activities have equivalent availability to be acted upon. Such a response will reinforce only a response of lesser strength. A major advantage of Premack's theory is that it construes reinforcement as a relation between a response and its consequences; that is, reinforcers are relative, not absolute. In addition, it yields an independent index of reinforcer strength through simple observation of the amount of time a subject spends doing a specific activity relative to other activities having potential for inclusion in one's behavioral repertoire. Of course, one could argue that reinforcement can be had through means other than an observable or empirically verifiable response; however, discussion of the ambiguities centering on issues in reinforcement theory is beyond the scope of this text.

In any event, Ayllon and Azrin (1965) used Premack's principle in arranging behaviors of high natural frequency in a program permitting the subjects to emit these behaviors at scheduled times. The operant technique requires delivery of a reinforcer only when a desired behavior occurs, immediately after the desired response is emitted; that is, the reinforcement is contingent upon the behavior.

In Experiment III an entire ward of 44 patients served as the subjects; their age range was 24–74 years, with a mean age of 51. These patients worked at various job assignments for tokens, which could be exchanged for such reinforcers as privacy, leave from the ward, social interaction with the staff, and recreational opportunites. In order to illustrate how important it is that reinforcement be contingent upon the desired behavior, Ayllon and Azrin presented tokens before the subjects' jobs were to begin and, after a few days had elapsed, their hours at work dropped off dramatically. When receipt of the tokens was once again made contingent upon completion of task assignments, working hours increased to the earlier levels (which had increased from the baseline rates derived from before the experiment began).

In short, these investigators utilized the age variable in operant conditioning by giving tokens, which could later be exchanged for whatever was individually rewarding, to groups of hospitalized patients when they emitted appropriate adaptive responses. The authors found no age limitations on the efficacy of the reinforcement contingencies, which were reported as related to an increase in adaptive behavior.

More recently, Baltes and Zerbe (1976) conducted a single subject study in which they hypothesized that an environmental change would result in change in a subject's self-feeding behavior. The subject was a 76-year-old female resident in a nursing home who exhibited such undesirable feeding behavior as dumping food and refusing to eat properly. The treatment approach involved continuous, immediate reinforcement of self-feeding and removal of reinforcers in a non-self-feeding condition when at the dining table (in addition, the Premack principle was applied). Results indicate that nonfeeding (an operant) can be changed to self-feeding as a function of (re)arranged environmental contingencies.

As stated, basic operant research with the elderly is sparse indeed because the bulk of the studies to date have used subjects other than the elderly. This is singularly important because generalizability to an older population is highly doubtful, as reported by Baltes and Barton (1977), who suggest that reinforcers effective for the young might not be so for the elderly. For example, money is a widely recognized, powerful secondary reinforcer for most people; however, some observers suggest that this holds true for those below the older adult level, but not for the elderly, for whom a variety of social reinforcers appear to be more effective than money.

We are already familiar with the dependencies concomitant with the advanced years. This typical condition has implications for the number, variety and frequency of reinforcers in the aged's environment. There is little doubt that the elderly's environment is characterized by the absence (through a wide range of losses) of stimulus (discriminative) settings through which behavior is rewarded. We are not suggesting, however, that potential, effective reinforcers are absent, but that they simply have either not been identified or those that have been are not being utilized adequately. In this connection, perhaps dependency behaviors related to learned needs should not be reinforced by individuals, agencies, and institutions, whereas independency responses should be.

Effective schedules of reinforcement would appear to be different for the older adult, whose concept of time has undergone change. For example, a periodic schedule of high response-reward ratio might be less effective in maintaining novel behavior or increasing response rates than a continuous schedule, since, for one reason, the older person's notion of far future has been somehow transformed into immediate future.

STATE VARIABLES

State variables in the human organism such as set or expectancy, motivation or arousal are critical factors in the analysis of task performance or behavior in general, since they can affect both the ability to discriminate among stimuli and the ability to form new associations between stimuli and responses.

Set

Learning set studies consider the relationship between performance in prior learning to performance in subsequent learning in order to determine whether or not the subject has learned how to learn. Harlow (1949) defined learning set as "learning how to learn a kind of problem, or transfer from problem to problem [p. 54]." He derived this notion from a series of experiments involving monkeys who learned a number of visual discrimination problems. He observed that, after having solved a number of similar but unrelated problems, their rate of learning increased over trials. Postman (1964) reported similar results for human subjects who learned serial and paired-associate word lists; performance increments were observed on subsequent tasks similar to those originally learned, as well as on other, unrelated tasks (unrelated in the sense that the solution of the original task was unrelated to the solution of the subsequent task in that one solution gave no information about the other solution).

The development of a set is a function of several factors, one of which is the extent of one's education. In other words, learning set seems to be an increasing function of one's educational background, in which learning strategies were developed and sustained over time through practice with tasks of a cognitive nature.

Birren (1964) suggests that learning set phenomena may be related to attention to stimuli and selection of relevant aspects or components of the stimulus situation. Insofar as one has the ability to concentrate attention on crucial elements of a learning task, performance increments are observed. The literature suggests that the elderly do not "learn how to learn" as well as younger subjects.

To test this learning set hypothesis, Monge (1969) conducted a paired associate study in which 40 females served as subjects. Twenty aged 60–69 and 20 aged 30–39 were randomly assigned to either a slow pace, 4 (anticipation) : 2 (inspection) second rate, or a fast pace (4 : 1 second rate) condition. Specifically, the study was designed to determine age related performance deficits in speed of response and in focusing attention upon the learning tasks. It was hypothesized that if the anticipation interval were held constant, then the younger subjects would outperform the older. In addition, if the hypothesized poorer performance was a function of concentration difficulties at the fast pace, then age differences would be less significant under a slower paced condition in which the older group had time to acclimate themselves to stimulus–response conditions (i.e., to form a learning set).

Results indicate that a main effect due to age was not significant. As predicted, a main effect due to pace, however, was significant. Data indicate significant improvement from the first to the sixth list in total omission and commission errors made by both groups. The best performance was by the older group at a slow pace, for which Monge offered no explanation. At any rate, the main purpose of the study was to demonstrate that not all response decrements are a function of learning set inefficiences but are also due to inadequate feedback contingencies or insufficient time to make a response.

Motivation

The relationship between learning and motivation is ambiguous since, as in learning, motivation is inferred from performance. Investigators generally agree that performance, either in cognitive tasks or in general, is a function of Learning X Motivation (Kimble, 1961); however, the process of establishing the amount of variance accounted for by each becomes unwieldy because of the enormous complexity of their interaction.

Motivation can be defined as organismic states that arouse, maintain, and direct behavior toward a goal object. Subsumed under motivation are drives and incentives; however, it is not the intent of this chapter to deal with the controversial issues surrounding such categories, since we are concerned with performance decrements in the aged as a function of motivation loss. Unfortunately, research on the effects of age on drive states is virtually nonexistent. The literature is sparse, also, on the effects of age on the interaction between learning and motivation.

At any rate, a drive serves to energize an organism toward a restricted class of goals. For example, the basic drive of hunger energizes the organism toward the goal of food (the procuring of which reduces the drive and is therefore presumably rewarding). An incentive refers to an extrinsic reward or expectation of a reward following a particular sequence of goal directed behavior.

Obviously, educational gerontology depends on general experimental and physiological psychology to provide evidence concerning the neural mechanisms involved in drive or motivational states. Research from this sector is crucial to our understanding of learning performance, since brain mechanisms are known to deteriorate with age and are therefore related to age changes in at least one important aspect of motivation.

Autonomic Arousal

Some investigators believe that the elderly are autonomically overaroused (anxious) in the experimental situation and that this condition partially accounts for their poorer performance in learning tasks, such as more omission errors in fast paced tasks. Eisdorfer (1968) has provided evidence for that conclusion. Despite these findings some investigators suggest that the aging person is under-aroused. These researchers would invoke and interpret the classical-conditioning studies as evidence for underarousal, since the aged do not respond well to these procedures, perhaps because of a neural responsivity problem.

Eisdorfer, Nowlin, and Wilkie (1970) have provided additional evidence concerning the increased autonomic arousal (anxiety level) associated with involvement in or performance on a learning task. In this study, propranolol (Inderal) was administered to 13 of 28 male subjects aged 60–78. Propranolol produces interference at receptor sites, thereby reducing the physiologic concomitants of central nervous system arousal; that is, the drug partially blocks end organ response to the autonomic nervous system (ANS). The level of free fatty acid (FFA) in blood plasma is one index of autonomic arousal utilized by the investigators in their analysis. As these levels increase, task performance decreases. It was hypothesized that, if arousal levels can be reduced through drug action, then increments in learning should be observed.

A serial learning paradigm in which subjects were to recall a list of eight words was used to test that hypothesis. The words were exposed at a 4-second interval with a 1-second interval between words. The dependent measure was the total number of errors divided into commission and omission. Results indicate fewer omission and commission errors among the drug group; however, the differences were not statistically significant. The between-group difference in total errors was statistically significant at the .05 level. The drug group registered a decrease in FFA level, with a slight rise during performance, whereas the placebo group registered higher levels of FFA, with a concomitant rise during performance. Interaction effects were highly significant ($F = 12.0, df = 7/175, p < .01$). As predicted, the performance of the drug group was better than that of the placebo group.

The investigators therefore interpreted their findings as support for the hypothesis that performance decrements are a partial function of factors other than changes in central nervous system structures. Namely, increased autonomic arousal accounts for a significant portion of the variance in the aged's performance decrements. They also drew attention to their findings that indicate performance increments in the elderly can be realized through introduction of chemicals which modify ANS state.

Prize Incentive Effects

In addition to the physiological aspects of motivation, I am also interested in the psychological aspects as affected by manipulation of reward contingencies. The literature related to the effects of incentive on performance suggest that a "powerful factor in the arousal and maintenance of behavior is the expectation of getting an extrinsic reward. Rewarding someone with money and/or other tokens is a pervasive phenomenon throughout our society because of the presumed efficiency of a reward system [Agruso, TenBrink, & Dunathan, 1976, p. 229]." The evidence for its efficacy is equivocal, however.

TenBrink, Dunathan, and Agruso (1976) found that extrinsic reward in the form of prize money for performance in paired associate learning tasks neutralized the effects of pictorial mediators in groups of college-aged subjects. Performance on paired associate tasks for subjects who had the benefit of pictorial mediators coupled with a probability of winning a prize ($10) was of significantly lower quality than that of subjects who were neither eligible for a prize nor had the benefit of the mediators. These findings are significant, for one reason, because of the widely held assumption that image mediators facilitate paired associate learning and other memory tasks. In addition, the authors suggest that a shift in attention from task to probability of getting a prize partially accounts for the decrement in performance. Apparently, the no-prize group was not distracted by the possibility of winning a prize, "which was a function of variables either within or beyond their control [p. 211]."

Weiner (1967) and Agruso, TenBrink, and Dunathan (1976) provide evidence to further illustrate the ambiguities related to incentive effects. In a series of studies Weiner had subjects learn sets of trigrams (three consonant letters) which were presented with varying color backgrounds of different monetary values. For example, one color had a value of 1¢ if correctly recalled, while another color had a 5¢ value if recalled correctly. Between trials subjects rehearsed (practiced) what they had learned. Results showed that high incentive consonants (e.g., 5¢) were better recalled than lower incentive consonants (e.g., 1¢). Weiner suggested that the results are a function of incentive effects on retention in memory.

Agruso *et al.* (1976), in a followup of an earlier study, found that performance on paired associate learning tasks is both a function of the students' ability, as indeed one would predict, and of the students' perceived probability of attaining a prize. In this study 60 college students were divided into high-, medium-, and low-ability groups and then were randomly assigned to one of three groups, a control group (no prize probability) and low and high prize-probability treatment groups.

Results indicate that performance scores were lowest for the low-ability group and highest for the high-ability group. Students' performance under high prize-probability conditions was highest overall, whereas the performance of students under low prize-probability was lowest. The overall distribution of scores was stable for both low- and middle-ability students but was reversed among high-ability students, for whom the highest performance scores were registered under low prize-probability conditions and the lowest performance scores under high prize-probability and control conditions.

Among subjects of low and middle ability, high prize-probability is related to an increment in performance scores. On the other hand, it was suggested that low prize-probability may have an enervating rather than a facilitating effect among the lower ability groups.

The authors concluded that the application of monetary rewards as incentives among low- and middle-ability students is facilitating only under conditions in which the rewards are easily attainable. Prizes seen as virtually unattainable are related to lower performance scores than those which would be predicted if the prize conditions were excluded. Among students of high ability, virtually unattainable prizes yield no significantly different effect from no prizes at all. The authors suggest that among students for whom the task represents an inadequate challenge, the addition of a prize incentive may increase interest in the task concomitant with an increase in effort.

Interpretation of these results suggests that token or incentive programs should be more precise in applying reinforcers to students for whom performance increments might be predicted and in avoiding application of reinforcers to those students whose performance would reflect decrements. Expressed differently, rewards have differential effects contingent upon ability and expectation.

These studies involved college-aged subjects; it would seem appropriate, then, to conduct similar studies with the elderly so that comparative data, which is nonexistent at this time, can be analyzed for age differences. This would appear especially important in light of efforts to design curricula for adults and learning experiences for the elderly that would maximize potential, since to accomplish this we need to know the kinds of reinforcers that facilitate learning performance in the elderly as well as the conditions under which they are functional.

I am inclined to believe that high- and low-ability groups could be distinguished among the elderly, the responsiveness of which to token programs or a reward system under learning performance conditions would parallel that of a younger group of divided abilities, and for similar reasons.

The literature indicates that the elderly do not perform as well as younger subjects on verbal learning tasks. Perhaps a significant factor, besides task meaningfulness, interest, instructions, etc., is their perceived probability of their not only completing the task but also of performing "well"; that is, of getting a reward of an intrinsic–extrinsic nature in both instances.

Response Inhibition. A case in point is provided by Taub (1967), who conducted a study in which 80 volunteer subjects, divided equally into groups of mean age 26.1 and 69.7, learned paired-associate lists to a criterion of 2 errorless trials or to a maximum of 30 trials, whichever came first. Two presentation rates were used, 4 or 8 seconds for the stimulus and 4 or 8 seconds for the S–R pairs. Groups were classified as either no response, for whom standard learning instructions were given, and required response, who were given the standard instructions and were also told that they must respond to each stimulus, even if they had to guess.

An analysis of total omission errors indicated that age, presentation rate, and Age X Rate were significant sources of variance. Analysis of commission errors indicated that age and presentation rate were significant. Response instructions did not have a measurable effect on either type of error. These results clearly show that both types of errors decreased with rate of presentation.

Taub interpreted these findings as evidence for a tendency on the part of the older subjects to inhibit responding despite instructions to respond in any event. The findings further indicate that the older subject failed to respond unless the probability (perceived or otherwise inferred in this study) of being correct was high. This held true even under the increased time of 8 seconds and with encouragement to respond, at least on the first trial. On the second trial, however, both types of errors for old and young were equal, indicating that, given ample practice time, the older subject will be more likely to respond.

In short, Taub (1967) submits that the aged tend to withhold responses, apparently as a partial function of the probability of being right. Stated differently, Taub suggests that the elderly will refrain from making a response unless there is a high probability of its being correct. Leech and Witte (1971) suggested that a portion of the omission errors committed by the elderly could be a function of their lack of confidence, as was earlier indicated by Taub (1967) and elaborated upon by Welford (1976), who suggests that learning performance is not only a function of abilities but also of willingness to expend the effort demanded if one is to work up to full potential.

Welford submits that perhaps the elderly are not so much unwilling but, instead, are more hesitant about taking action than their younger counterparts. In addition, they seem to be more cautious than younger persons, a conclusion derived from data showing a tendency to accumulate redundant information before making a decision or taking action. These factors apparently affect the speed with which the elderly learn and the nature of what is actually learned, since withholding responses certainly affects one's knowledge about what was not responded to; that is, the knowledge of results gives information that can serve as new input or can modify old input. Welford aptly points out that unwillingness to emit a response unless one is certain about its correctness results in possible failure to use effectively what has been learned.

Reinforcement Expectancies

The bulk of the research dealing with the effects of incentive on performance has been conducted with children and college students as subjects. However, Leech (1974) compared the performance of elderly and young adults on skill and chance tasks. She hypothesized that the performance of the elderly is a function of low expectancies for success and high expectancies that many events are beyond their ability to control. Results supported the hypothesis that the elderly group had lower generalized expectancies than the younger group. The implications for social learning theory were pointed out (which are not unrelated to the findings of Agruso *et al.*, 1976). It would seem that changing the expectancies of the aged from failure to success is a challenging problem for future research.

Verbal Incentive Effects

Hutchinson (1973) compared the performance of 54 young and 54 elderly subjects in a two-choice verbal discrimination task. Following each response subjects received feedback in the form of praise or reproof or "right" and "wrong." Results indicate no significant age differences as a function of feedback. Best performance for all subjects was reported under the "right" condition and under the "neutral" condition in which the experimenter remained silent when a wrong response was given. Under praise and reproof conditions, the performance of the younger subjects was best when a neutral approach was used and poorest when praise was given. The performance of the older subjects was equal across praise, reproof, and neutral treatment conditions.

Kausler and Lair (1968) had earlier conducted a verbal discrimination study in which 48 subjects were divided into three goups of mean ages 66.9, 69.6, and 68.3 to perform under three conditions, right–wrong (RW), in which the subject is informed whether the response given is right or wrong; right–nothing (RN), in which the experimenter tells the subject of right responses but remains silent when a wrong response is emitted; and wrong–nothing (WN), in which the experimenter informs of wrong responses but says nothing when right responses are given by the subject. The subjects learned 12 pairs of words to 1 perfect trial or to a maximum of 15 trials, whichever occurred first. The pairs were presented at a 4-second rate; the interitem interval was 4 seconds, and the intertrial interval was 8 seconds.

Results indicate no significant differences among the three conditions up to trial 6; however, from that point on performance of the WN group was poorer than that of the RW and RN groups. This trend in mean error performance was found to be statistically significant among reinforcement conditions. According to these investigators, the "wrong" feedback cues were perceptually isolated because they were the only form of reinforcement present, which apparently resulted in perseveration of wrong choices instead of leading to their omission on subsequent trials. The authors pointed out that this may be a function of the aging process itself, since it is not found in younger subjects.

In short, Kausler and Lair (1968) found that older subjects perseverated wrong choices under the "wrong" feedback condition when similar discrimination tasks were used. It is interesting to note that verbal praise incentive with an elderly group had effects similar to those reported by Agruso *et al.* (1976) in which younger subjects were used with prize incentives. Again, it becomes increasingly clear that across the board dispensing of rewards is inefficient, to say the least.

Another study related to that of Hutchinson (1973) had been conducted earlier by Lair and Moon (1972). In this study, 33 elderly and 33 middle-aged male subjects were divided and assigned to conditions as follows: Elderly—praise (mean age 66), reproof (mean age 65.6), control (mean age 67.4). Middle aged—praise (mean age 40.8), reproof (mean age 40.1), control (mean age 43). After five trials involving a modified digit–symbol task, the subjects were given the incentive feedback. The praise groups were informed of their good performance, the reproof subjects were told of their poor performance, and the control groups were asked to be patient while their tasks were being graded. Following this first feedback condition, another five trials were completed using the same procedure. A final five trials followed.

Results indicated that the performance of the elderly was below that of the middle-aged under both positive and negative feedback conditions. The reproof condition is related to the poorest performance for the elderly. The performance increments realized by the elderly during the early trials under the praise condition dissipated over the 15 trials. Performance increments held across the three trial blocks under control (neutral) condition. Differences between fast and slow responders indicate that the elderly fast show decrement after reproof while the middle-aged slow show increment. These findings are generally consistent with those of Kausler and Lair (1968).

VERBAL LEARNING

> Learning is a cumulative process. The more knowledge and skills an individual acquires, the more likely it becomes that his new learning will be shaped by his past experiences and activities. An adult rarely, if ever, learns anything completely new; however unfamiliar the task that confronts him, the information and habits he has built up in the past will be his point of departure. Thus transfer of training from old to new situations is part and parcel of most, if not all, learning. In this sense the study of transfer is coextensive with the investigation of learning. However, it is only when the conditions of prior training are brought under experimental control that the contributions of transfer can be precisely evaluated [Postman, 1972, p. 1019].

Since learning performance theories are derived from verbal learning models out of which comes data on the acquisition, retention, and transfer of learned associations under controlled conditions, we will consider representative studies in adult learning that attempt to explain and describe these processes.

Although verbal learning presumably measures "raw" learning, there is little question that past habit and prior learning interact with retention of material presented in paired associate, free- and serial-recall tasks. Therefore, it would seem useful to make a distinction between verbal learning and verbal behavior. Let the former refer to the acquisition of associations (e.g., S–R pairs) and the latter to the actual performance of that which has been acquired (e.g., learned associations). What we have then is a distinction that parallels (more or less) the one suggested for learning and performance under other contingencies.

The reader should also recognize the problem in generalizing from simple laboratory controlled conditions to enormously complex natural situations. To the extent that explanatory factors determined in the laboratory transfer or generalize to more complex conditions, so much the better for the verbal learning model.

Interference

As Birren (1964) points out, interference effects are an increasing function of one's age and cumulative experiences. Related to this is the fact that positive and negative transfer in subsequent learning conditions is seen to increase as a function of one's experiential background.

Kay (1967) explains that transfer had traditionally been treated as a distinct problem by researchers in learning, contrary to his observation that "all learning is an example of transfer insofar as one learning situation is never identical with another, even in the controlled Pavlovian experiments [p. 632]." Hence, the distinction between transfer and adult learning is at best tenuous (Kay, 1967). The literature up to this time indicates that interference is a function of aging, to the extent that, as one ages, one becomes more susceptible to its effects. The literature also suggests that the evidence for increased retroaction effects with age is equivocal; that is, that interference effects resulting from the acquisition of new material on the recall or relearning of older material increase during the adult years. In any case, we will treat interference as an aspect of the transfer problem.

Gladis and Braun (1958) conducted a study to determine age differences in retroactive interference effects and transfer. In this study, 120 subjects were assigned to three age groups of 40 each, with age ranges of 20–29, 40–49, and 60–72. Each subject learned two 8-item lists of paired associates (e.g., "HX" as stimulus item, "winding" as response item, which represents an example in the original learning list) to the criterion of one errorless trial. The paired associates were presented at a rate of 4 seconds for the stimulus and 4 seconds for the S–R pair. The intertrial interval was 8 seconds. Following the original learning task, each subject learned another 8-item list in which the stimulus item remained the same while the response item changed; that is, their similarity varied from high to neutral. This corresponds roughly to the A–B, A–C paradigm.

The results indicate significant differences in amount of positive transfer among the groups. Retroaction decreased as a function of the similarity between response items of original learning and interpolated learning. Of particular significance is the fact that, when adjustments were made for differences in initial vocabulary level and in the ability to learn, no significant differences in retroaction were found, which is at variance with the findings of Wimer and Wigdor (1958). The degree to which the initial task is learned thus relates to the amount of difference among the groups so' that, as original task learning increases, interference decreases.

Arenberg (1967) hypothesized that age differences in retroaction would be a function of the duration of the anticipation interval to the extent that differences at longer intervals would be negligible. In his study, 48 subjects divided into a young group (age range 30.0–39.1) and an old group (age range 62.8–77.5) were assigned to short- or long-anticipation-interval conditions. Test items and procedures were similar to those used in the Gladis and Braun study. The anticipation interval for the fast groups was 1.9 seconds and for the slow groups 3.7 seconds. Inspection interval was 1.9 seconds for all subjects. Age differences were reported in relearning at short but not at long anticipation intervals. The findings of this study were interpreted as supportive of his hypothesis.

Hulicka (1967) tested the hypothesis that when task materials are learned to the same criterion of mastery, no significant age differences in interference effects from interpolated learning would be found. Eighty subjects divided into mean age groups of 70 and 15 years participated in this study, the findings of which were consistent with her hypothesis.

In sum, Hulicka (1967) and Arenberg (1967) conducted studies in which the anticipation interval was slightly shorter (Arenberg) or slightly longer (Hulicka) than the 4-second condition of Gladis and Braun (1958); however, similar results were reported in each study; that is, a short anticipation interval is related to higher interference effects for the elderly to the extent that, the longer the interval (within limits), the better the performance for the elderly. Arenberg (1973) points out that the high-interference models used by these investigators produced more retroaction effects in both groups and that the results of these studies are not unequivocal.

Traxler and Britton (1970) conducted a study to determine the nature of interference as an age-related factor. This study differed somewhat from the preceding studies in that anticipation intervals were varied and, in addition, different transfer models were used. A written, modified method of free recall was employed to measure original learning. They hypothesized that the performance of the older group would reflect more retroactive inhibition (RI) than that of the younger group under the three transfer conditions and that "the largest age differences in RI would be under negative transfer conditions and that age differences in RI would be magnified under the fast pace (short anticipation interval) condition [p. 683]."

The 120 male subjects were divided into groups of mean age 27.42 and 68.73. Each subject learned lists (original and interpolated) of eight two-syllable adjectives in which two anticipation intervals were used, 2 seconds and 4 seconds for fast and slow pace, respectively. The three transfer conditions were: AB–AC, AB–CB, and AB–CD.

The findings of this study were interpreted as supportive of the hypotheses. The authors suggested that the older group's performance reflected more RI than that of the younger group because of the difficulty "experienced with advancing age in shifting from one cognitive set to another [p. 684]." Specifically, the older subject displayed greater difficulty in shifting from AB to AC, which indicates that there was more for the older group to "unlearn" (which of course was found in their lower recall of original learning).

Language and Retroaction

Canestrari (1966) suggests that the Gladis and Braun (1958) study provides indirect evidence in support of an interference hypothesis, since the 60–72 age group exhibited less positive transfer than the 20–29 group. To provide a more direct test of that hypothesis, Canestrari (1966) designed a study in which the language habits (which presumably interfere in the formation of new word associations) of subjects were determined before experimentation began. To determine preexisting linguistic habits, each subject was given the Kent–Rosanoff Word Association Test, based on the results of which groups were divided into young (high and low commonality) and old (high and low commonality). Level of commonality is determined by the number of responses given to stimulus words. High commonality is defined by the number of common responses and low commonality by the number of unique responses.

The 120 subjects used in this study were divided into groups of 60 elderly with mean age of 65.73 and 60 young with mean age of 16.77 years. Subjects were then randomly assigned to groups who learned 10-word paired associate lists of high or low associative strength under self-paced conditions to criterion of one perfect trial.

Results of analysis of covariance indicate a significant main effect due to age ($p < .001$) and to list ($p < .001$); significant Age × List and Commonality × List interactions ($p < .005$ and $p < .025$, respectively). Nonsignificant Age × Commonality and Age × Commonality × List interactions were found.

The author hypothesized that if preexisting language habits contribute to more interference for the elderly, as suggested in the literature, then the elderly high commonality should exhibit poorer performance than that of young high commonality. The elderly low commonality should not exhibit any disability to the same extent.

Canestrari (1966) concluded that, although linguistic habits did affect performance, "young and elderly subjects experienced the same relative degree of interference or facilitation in learning the lists. The hypothesis of increased interference stemming from pre-existing habits was not supported [p. 7]."

Pacing

Experimental research provides compelling evidence that fast pacing in serial and paired associate learning is related to performance decrements in the elderly (Arenberg, 1965, 1973; Canestrari, 1963; Eisdorfer, Axelrod & Wilkie, 1963; Monge & Hultsch, 1971; Taub, 1967; Witte, 1975). A consistent finding is an Age X Anticipation Interval interaction (Arenberg, 1965), and not an Age X Inspection Interval one. Performance increments across the age span are observed under increased inspection intervals (Monge, 1969).

In an earlier systematic study of the pacing variable, Canestrari (1963) demonstrated that self-pacing is related to better performance in the aged than is experimental pacing. In this study, 30 males of age range 60-69 (mean age of 65.4), and 30 males of age range 17–35 (mean age of 23.9) served as subjects. Each subject learned all of three paired associate lists of six pairs under all of three conditions, which involved presentation rates of 1.5 and 3 seconds for the paced conditions and a self-paced condition in which the subject could use as much study and response time as desired.

Results indicated that the aged group did indeed realize better performance under the self-paced conditions; however, their performance was below that of the younger group for all three conditions. A signficant decrease in errors of omission were reported in the aged group, whereas commission errors for this group were stable across conditions. Comparisons of these errors at fast paces suggest performance rather than learning deficits. The author suggests that the pacing variable and the aged's inability to respond within the time limits of fast pace conditions account for a significant portion of the variance in performance decrements; that is, decrement is more a function of these factors than of a learning deficit.

In agreement with Eisdorfer, Axelrod, and Wilkie (1963), I am not interpreting comparative analyses of kinds of errors as a resolution of the learning–performance problem. It would seem that at least some of the errors observed under fast paced conditions are a function of learning deficits, since, for one reason, age differences are still observed under self-paced conditions (Arenberg, 1965), and increased exposure time is related at some point to decrement, rather than increment, in performance (Eisdorfer et al., 1963).

At any rate, Arenberg (1965) conducted two paired associate studies, one of which provides evidence in support of a learning deficit. The author alternated paced trials with self-paced trials. In addition, the anticipation interval (which was varied) was independent of the inspection interval. Results of Study II indicate performance decrements for the aged under the fast paced condition (1.9 second anticipation interval). An Age × Pace interaction was found under both paced and self-paced conditions. Differences between paced and self-paced errors were small. These data suggest that "few of the paced errors, even for the old group at the fast pace, can be attributed to insufficient time to emit a correctly learned response [Arenberg, 1965, p. 424]."

Wilkie and Eisdorfer (1977) reported a serial learning study in which differences related to sex, verbal ability, and pacing were examined among 64 male and female subjects with a mean age of 69.0 years. The authors used a 2 × 2 × 2 factorial design, in which the independent variables were sex, stimulus pacing speed of 4 and 10 seconds, and vocabulary level as determined by the vocabulary subtest of the Wechsler Adult Intelligence Scale (WAIS). Subjects were divided into average and high ability groups on the basis of their scaled scores on the WAIS.

Participants learned lists of eight five-letter disyllabic words of high association value. The procedure included stimulus exposure times of 4 and 10 seconds, 1-second interstimulus interval, 40-second intertrial interval, and learning criterion defined by 2 consecutive perfect trials, or to a limit of 15 trials. Subjects were divided into an Average Vocabulary Group and High Vocabulary Group; eight men and eight women from each group learned under the 4-second and 10-second pacing speeds.

Results indicate that performance of the average elderly male at fast pacing was below their performance at slower speeds, thereby supporting earlier findings reported in the literatrue. The authors suggest that the average male performance at the fast pace was a function of more omission errors (i.e., they emitted fewer responses). There were no significant differences in the number of commission errors.

The authors made particular note of the fact that the average elderly female emitted more responses at the fast pace. Their performance approached that of high verbal male and female.

There were no sex differences at the 10-second pacing condition. At the 10-second pace the average verbal male increased his response rate and therefore realized a performance increment.

In sum, the performance of the average verbal male at the fast pace was below that of the average verbal female. The average male gains at the slow pace were higher than that of the other groups. Verbal fluency and verbal ability along with rapid response rates were suggested as accounting for a significant portion of variance in sex differences at the fast pace.

Total Time

Thus far we have examined studies of age differences under paired associate procedures in which anticipation and inspection intervals have been of equal duration or in which the inspection interval has been varied while the anticipation interval was held constant and vice versa. Monge and Hultsch (1971) suggest that these intervals have not been independently varied and that emphasis has been on the anticipation interval. The studies report a significant interaction between age and presentation rate, presumably as a function of the relatively poor comparative performance of older and young subjects. These researchers therefore conducted a study to determine the effects of anticipation and inspection interval variation.

The subjects in the study were 72 white males divided into age groups of 20–39 and 40–66 years. Both the anticipation and inspection intervals were 2.2, 4.4, and 6.6 seconds. Each subject learned a 10-item paired associate list of noun as stimulus and adjective as response.

Results indicate that age interacts with anticipation interval, but no significant interaction was found with inspection interval; also, performance increments were observed for all ages as inspection interval increased from 2.2 to 4.4 seconds, all of which is consistent with the findings of the other investigations discussed earlier.

The Monge and Hultsch study is also interesting in that the results indicate that the "two intervals interact neither with each other nor jointly with age [p. 161]." These data can be interpreted to mean that the total time available per item (i.e., anticipation plus inspection interval time) is not differentially important to subjects of different ages. It is the proportion of total time used in the anticipation interval that accounts for the significant age differences.

Winn and Elias (1975) applied the total time principle (Bugelski, 1962) to the data of Monge and Hultsch (1971) in order to test a hypothesis that the total time needed to learn a task will not differ significantly, despite variable presentation rates (i.e., the total time needed to learn serial and paired associate word lists, regardless of time intervals, is the same). Their reinterpretation of the Monge and Hultsch data supports the total time principle.

Strength of Associations

Botwinick (1973) reviewed the more recent literature relating to the meaningfulness of the verbal tasks administered to the elderly under experimentally controlled conditions. He suggested that although performance increments are observed in the aged when the task materials are meaningful or organized for learning, their performance is nonetheless below that of younger groups. However, there are exceptions for the high verbal aged, the implications of which will be discussed in Chapter 5.

For our purposes, meaningfulness will be discussed in the context of associative strength. The derivation of association strength is in word association sampling, as discussed earlier in the Canestrari (1966) study. You will recall that age differences for the high associative strength word pairs were lower than age differences for low strength pairs. These findings are consistent with those of Kausler and Lair (1966), who, in addition, reported that elderly subjects profited more than younger subjects from high associative strength pairs. These latter investigators compared the acquisition rates of young and old subjects who learned lists of nine paired words rated as high, low, or zero associative strength. The results indicate that the performance of the older group was significantly below that of the younger group on low pairs only. These observers suggest that differences in acquisition rates as a function "of pre-existing associative strength may be related to increasing age from early maturity on, and may become more pronounced during old age [p. 280]." The findings of this study are also consistent with those of Zaretsky and Halberstam (1968a).

Zaretsky and Halberstam (1968b) conducted a study to determine the relationship between aging, brain damage, and verbal learning in 102 hospitalized subjects who were divided into four groups of 30 elderly (age range 60–85) brain damaged, 30 elderly non-brain damaged, 12 young (20–45 age range) brain damaged, and 30 young non-brain damaged. Each subject learned three five-word pairs of high, medium, and low associative strengths on 3 consecutive days. Response time was 10 seconds. After criterion was reached, each subject performed nonverbal tasks for 15 minutes, at which time the relearning phase began under the same conditions as the original learning.

Results indicate that, in terms of response latency, the elderly groups performed at slower rates than the younger groups under all levels of word association strength. During relearning, a slight decrease in differences for response latency and trials to criterion under all association levels was indicated. There were significant differences among the experimental groups for trials to learning and relearning criterion for age and associative strength.

These investigators point out that the significant factor accounting for performance differences was age, not brain damage. Performance increments were related to level of associative strength. Performance was poorest for all subjects under the low association condition.

The authors interpret these results as corroboration of the assumption that elderly subjects profit from preexisting learning insofar as it relates (is meaningful) to the present task; however, and perhaps more importantly, they encounter relatively more difficulty in the learning of new word associations. Thus, their findings favor a learning deficit explanation related to age.

On the other hand, Wittels (1972) raises the question of whether meaningful verbal materials are equally meaningful for all age groups in light of the fact that the connotative and denotative aspects of words are in an apparent state of flux within and across generations. She therefore hypothesized that under conditions of equally meaningful stimuli, age related deficits in recall would be neutralized.

One hundred two female subjects were equally divided into a young group (mean age 19.7) and an older group (mean age 70.0). Each subject learned lists of 15 stimulus words from the Kent–Rosanoff selection. The final word pairs were constructed so that all pairs were operationally equal in meaningfulness to all subjects. Paired associate exposure time was 4 seconds for the first trial. From the second trial through criterion or to a maximum of 15 trials, the stimulus word was exposed for 4 seconds. The interitem interval was 1 second, and the intertrial interval was 10 seconds.

Analyses of variance in total errors and trials to criterion showed a significant age effect ($p < .0001$). This was the only significant effect obtained. The absolute number of paired associates recalled was fewer for the older group than for the younger. The older group also made more mean errors than the younger subjects and required more mean trials than the younger group.

Wittles concluded that meaningfulness as defined in this study did not account for a significant portion of the age related variance in learning performance; in other words, the hypothesis was not supported. She suggested that perhaps meaningfulness is unimportant in comparative analyses of performance on paired associate tasks. She further submitted that perhaps the rapid pacing, in addition to the length of the paired associate list, related to the relatively poor performance of these elderly subjects. Winn, Elias, and Marshall (1976) reported findings consistent with those of Wittels (1972).

Finally, the interpretation of the absence of an Age × Condition interaction for error scores indicates that preexisting language is not a significant factor in accounting for interference effects in the elderly, which is a finding similar to that of Canestrari (1966).

REACTION TIME

An enormous amount of research has been published that provides compelling evidence for an invariant decline in speed of response and reaction time under a wide variety of conditions as one ages; that is, as age increases, speed of response decreases (Birren, 1974; Botwinick, 1973; Eisdorfer & Lawton, 1973; Palmore, 1970, 1974). Changes in the nervous system such as cell loss, slowing of peripheral nerve functions, and changes in synaptic transmission have been suggested as accounting for the slowing of behavior (Shock, 1962). However, as research designs become more sophisticated, some of the reported significance of age differences is attenuated.

The role and importance of response speed and reaction time in cognitive functions is discussed as appropriate throughout the book. At this point there is one very important study that deserves mention, since it has focused attention on the undesirability of accepting categorically the slowing of response rate as a fixed phenomenon in the aged.

Botwinick (1967) conducted studies in which comparative analyses of the response rates of young and old athletes indicated that indeed the older subjects had slower response rates, as predicted. However, when the reaction time performance of the older athletes was compared to that of younger nonathletes, the significance of slower reaction time did not prevail. The author suggested that in future reaction time studies both individual differences and exercise habits should be considered.

According to Botwinick (1973), despite the evidence relating changes in central nervous system mechanisms to the slowing of behavior with age, the relationship of this phenomenon to learning and cognate functioning is indeed ambiguous. He suggests that exercise programs and motivational states can neutralize the degree of decline in rate of responding. As to the aspect of individual differences, he states that "Very many old people are quicker in responding than many young adults [p. 177]."

In sum, the literature discussed thus far indicates that elderly subjects sustained performance decrements under rapid pace conditions in verbal learning tasks, especially under the paired associate paradigm, whereas performance increments were realized under slower pace conditions. One could interpret these findings to mean that the elderly require (perhaps because of a decline in the efficiency of CNS mechanisms) more time to emit a correct response under the contrived conditions of a laboratory, in which a multiplicity of other factors, such as anxiety, motivation, etc., interact to affect dependent measures. Some would suggest, therefore, that even in natural situations outside the laboratory the elderly should be given more time, relative to the young person, to perform any task, learning or otherwise. The extent to which they need additional time is an unresolved issue.

RESEARCH TRENDS AND ISSUES IN ADULT LEARNING AND MEMORY

An enormous amount of research published over the past 20 years indicates that the elderly simply do not learn as well as young persons and that memory declines as a function of increasing age. A number of theories and hypotheses have been advanced to account for the performance decrements found among the aged; one such focuses on the loss of neurons over time, which is related to less than optimal CNS functioning. Some observers have suggested that the cumulative effects of interference, lack of motivation, and a range of perceptual changes which are related to inadequate registration of stimulus events result in inefficient retention. Eisdorfer (1975), having conducted a number of studies in adult verbal learning, suggests that the decrements reported in the literature on aging are largely a function of performance variables and that, therefore, the

precise nature of the learning deficit is simply unknown. He submits that autonomic nervous system processes and performance factors contribute to a significant portion of the variance in the elderly's learning deficit, and, short of a better understanding of these variables, we are unable to define authentic learning
deficits.

Organismic-Intervening Factors

Most of the studies demonstrating an age related decrement in learning performance tasks have been cross-sectional, in which a comparative analysis of performance by persons of varied ages on identical tasks is rendered. Hulicka (1975)
suggests that perhaps persons who differ in chronological age also differ in other
variables such as physiological state, sensory acuity, and learning sets. She further suggests that differences in retention scores might be a function of differences in amount perceived and learned, as well as differences in memory processes such as registration and retrieval and atmosphere for recall, to name just
a few. Given inferential intervening processes involving learning and memory
mechanisms between stimulus input and response output, the evidence for irreversible, inevitable decrement in behavior is inconclusive, according to Hulicka.

These enormously complex intervening processes are likely influenced by
other factors, the nature of which are ambiguous. Recognizing this, some investigators are not using age as an independent variable but rather are interested in
identifying factors accounting for variance at one or more phases (such as registration or association) of the S–R continuum. They are focusing research efforts
(notwithstanding the methodological difficulties involved in dealing in comparable groups) on age related interactions in an attempt to explain the antecedents of differences rather than merely to describe conditions. The reader should
be particularly alert to problem areas and issues discussed here and throughout
the book, since their resolution is essential both in the design of learning–memory
studies which would yield definitive results and in the accurate interpretation of
age differences and age changes derived from the research already reported in the
literature.

Hulicka (1975) submits that a high priority area of research should be the
biochemical, neurological aspects of memory, since it is conceivable that these
dimensions account for a significant portion of the variability related to differences in memory functions among diverse age groups.

Methodological Considerations

Methodological considerations should include the development of stimulus
materials and experimental procedures amenable to older groups, since much of
what is utilized now has been standardized on young subjects. Learning per-

formance scores are undoubtedly related to the total context in which subjects are tested. An aspect of this situation has been investigated by Howell (1975), who suggested that older subjects in the typical, contrived laboratory setting are confronted with task materials and procedures virtually meaningless and unfamiliar to them. It would appear, then, that performance decrements are, to a considerable degree, a function of these environmental conditions.

In this connection, Howell (1975) conducted a study in which 48 persons of mean age 28.39 and 48 persons of mean age 68.52 were given a variety of perceptual recognition tests that varied in degree of familiarity and meaningfulness. She hypothesized that perceptual recognition scores are a function of level of meaningfulness and familiarity of stimulus materials. In addition, she hypothesized that older subjects' performance will reflect more decrement than that of younger subjects, but that the deficits (if any) would be least for task materials most familiar and meaningful to older subjects. A final hypothesis is that the degree of contextual complexity of the stimulus materials would be related to more recognition errors in the older group.

Meaningfulness was defined in terms of the stimulus materials' anticipated relevance and affective interest and the extent to which stimuli were otherwise generationally appropriate to the subjects (i.e., relevant in the sense that the stimulus item has practical application in real life situations). Familiarity was defined in terms of frequency of exposure to similar materials. Recency and context of exposure were also part of the definition, since the context in which a frequent, familiar item is observed has generational properties that make it more recognizable to one group than to another.

The results were consistent with the hypotheses and were interpreted to suggest that one factor of familiarity that differentiates stimuli for subjects is their contextual placement; that is, a common stimulus item presented out of context and in a complex way will be related to performance decrements for the elderly, more than for their younger counterparts. Thus, research designs should define the differentiating characteristics of objects and environments idiosyncratic to a given generation. In short, Howell believes that the older subject has more ability than performance scores reflect and can therefore perform well on highly complex tasks presented in a familiar setting.

Retention and Inhibition

A problem area receiving considerable attention is that of the interference proneness of the aged, discussed by Goulet (1975) within the context of degree of learning, mediated versus nonmediated learning, and response time.

He points out that equating for degree of learning is essential in establishing an age related decrement; that is, before a true deficit can be ascertained the materials to be learned must be equally "available." One solution to this problem of degree of learning is to have all subjects perform to the same criterion of mastery on the stimulus materials. However, whether or not reaching a particular criterion indicates true learning is a moot question. Goulet (1975) suggests an alternate method which involves the presentation of the material to be learned over a constant number of trials for all subjects, despite the fact that this method does not assume an interaction between degree of learning and age (which, of course, is questionable itself). In short, the research in this problem area should be directed toward identifying the antecedent age related mechanisms and processes, because degree of learning influences performance.

Although the use of mediators in retention tasks is discussed in succeeding chapters, I would like to suggest that mediated and nonmediated learning is a critical class of variables in the study of learning processes, one that needs further exploration. There is compelling evidence that the use of mnemonic devices is related to performance increments in both young and old subjects, but that their spontaneous utilization tends to decline after the middle years. It would appear that procedures involving instructions to use mediators during the acquisition process would serve to equate both degree and type of learning, since their differential usage by young and old is most likely related to retention score differences.

A number of studies reported earlier indicate that the performance decrements of the aged are a function of response time; that is, the deficits are due to the fast pace of experimental tasks. When the pace is slowed, performance increments are observed. Goulet (1975) suggests that the use of paced recall tests, in which an Age X Anticipation Interval interaction is found, may in fact reflect "performance differences that were also measured during acquistion, real differences related to retention or retroaction, or both [p. 189]." However, insofar as exposure intervals in acquistion and retention stages are manipulated independently, the foregoing limitations are somewhat neutralized.

SUMMARY REMARKS

The foregoing discussion does not purport to have exhausted the research findings in the area of adult human learning. Rather, I have been highly selective, restricting my treatment to those organismic variables and task variables which should be of particular interest to those involved in educational gerontology at this point in its evolution. The variables discussed have immediate importance and the study of them should form the basis out of which principle is at some point related to practice.

Several hypotheses were discussed which account, in varying degrees, for the difference in age related decrements under verbal learning conditions. The real issue, of course, is how much of the variance is a function of performance variables and how much is due to learning deficits. The controversy is unresolved at this time; however, I am inclined to believe that performance factors alone or in interaction with other task variables cannot account for all the age differences in verbal learning. At least some of that variance is a function of a learning disability. The evidence is strong that the elderly just do not learn, in quantitative or qualitative terms or both, within equal time limits, what young subjects do. The dynamic processes involved in this learning deficit, which may or may not be reversible, are fruitful areas for research.

Results from manipulation of the pace variable provide the strongest support for performance rather than learning deficits. Investigators have varied both the anticipation and the inspection intervals; they find, consistently, that as anticipation time increases, elderly performance scores are observed to increase. Similarly, if the anticipation interval is decreased, there is a corresponding response decrement in the aged. Some researchers suggest that the elderly need more time to respond than what is given under a fast pace condition in a laboratory setting. Under a self-paced condition, for example, performance is observed to approach and in some cases to equal or excel the performance of young subjects.

The enormously complex phenomenon of motivation is a significant factor, distinct from yet interacting with learning ability, in learning performance. The elderly have been observed as being overaroused in verbal learning settings, which results in a measurable level of anxiety which, in turn, was hypothesized as contributing to both inhibited performance and withheld responses, presumably because of fear of failure, stemming from lack of confidence. The effects of the circularity of this phenomenon is believed to account for a significant portion of the variance in dependent measures under conditions of verbal learning. When heightened arousal is reduced either by drugs or by other means, such as informative feedback contingencies, performance increments are observed.

The elderly seem to have lower generalized expectancies of success, which was observed as having an effect on task performance in particular and willingness to respond in general. There is a tendency for the elderly to inhibit responses unless there is a high probability that the response is right and is thereby, by extension, reinforcing.

Performance increments were observed as an increasing function of associative strength. The performance of all subjects was observed to improve as the task becomes more meaningful. There is some question, however, as to the nature of meaningfulness in the verbal learning paradigm, since words take on meanings idiosyncratic to a generation, each of which adapts, through the use of language, to rapidly changing contingencies.

REFERENCES

AGRUSO, V. M. JR., TENBRINK, T. D., & DUNATHAN, A. T. Paired associate task performance effects of ability and perceived prize probability. *Contemporary Educational Psychology*, 1976, *1*, 229–235.

ARENBERG, D. Anticipation interval and age differences in verbal learning. *Journal of Abnormal and Social Psychology*, 1965, *70*, 419–425.

ARENBERG, D. Age differences in retroaction. *Journal of Gerontology*, 1967, *22*, 88–91.

ARENBERG, D. Cognition and aging: Verbal learning, memory and problem solving. In C. Eisdorfer & M. Lawton (Eds.), *The psychology of adult development and aging*. Washington, D.C.: American Psychological Association, 1973.

AYLLON, T., & AZRIN, N. H. The measurement and reinforcement of behavior of psychotics. *Journal of Experimental Analysis of Behavior*, 1965, *8*, 357–383.

BALTES, M. M., & ZERBE, M. B. Re-establishing self-feeding in a nursing home resident. *Nursing Research*, 1976, *25*, 24–26.

BALTES, M. M., & BARTON, E. M. New approaches toward aging: A case for the operant model. *Educational Gerontology: An International Quarterly*, 1977, *2*, 383–405.

BALTES, P. B., & GOULET, L. R. Status and issues of a life-span developmental psychology. In L. R. Goulet & P. B. Baltes (Eds.), *Life-span developmental psychology: Research and theory*. New York: Academic Press, 1970.

BIRREN, J. E. *The psychology of aging*. Englewood Cliffs, New Jersey: Prentice-Hall, 1964.

BIRREN, J. E. Translations in gerontology — From lab to life. *American Psychologist*, 1974, *29*, 11, 808–815.

BOTWINICK, J. *Cognitive processes in maturity and old age*. New York: Springer, 1967.

BOTWINICK, J. Learning in children and in older adults. In L. R. Goulet & Paul B. Baltes (Eds.), *Life-span developmental psychology: Research and theory*. New York: Academic Press, 1970.

BOTWINICK, J. *Aging and behavior: A comprehensive integration of research findings*. New York: Springer, 1973.

BRAUN, H. W., & GEISELHART. Age differences in the acquisition and extinction of the conditioned eyelid response. *Journal of Experimental Psychology*, 1959, *57*, 386–388.

BUGELSKI, B. R. Presentation time, total time, and mediation in paired-associate learning. *Journal of Experimental Psychology*, 1962, *63*, 409–412.

CANESTRARI, R. E. Paced and self paced learning in young and elderly adults. *Journal of Gerontology*, 1963, *18*, 165–168.

CANESTRARI, R. E. Effects of commonality on paired associate learning in two age groups. *Journal of Genetic Psychology*, 1966, *108*, 3–7.

EISDORFER, C. Arousal and performance: Verbal learning. In G. A. Talland (Ed.), *Human aging and behavior*. New York: Academic Press, 1968.

EISDORFER, C. New dimensions and a tentative theory. In D. B. Lumsden & R. H. Sherron (Eds.), *Experimental studies in adult learning and memory*. Washington, D.C.: Hemisphere Publishing, 1975.

EISDORFER, C., AXELROD, S., & WILKIE, F. Stimulus exposure time as a factor in serial learning in an aged sample. *Journal of Abnormal and Social Psychology*, 1963, *67*, 594–600.

EISDORFER, C., NOWLIN, J., & WILKIE, F. Improvement of learning in the aged by modification of autonomic nervous system activity. *Science*, 1970, *170*, 1327–1329.

EISDORFER, C., & LAWTON, M. P. (Eds.). *The psychology of adult development and aging*. Washington, D.C.: American Psychological Association, 1973.

GLADIS, M., & BRAUN, H. W. Age differences in transfer and retroaction as function of intertask response similarity. *Journal of Experimental Psychology*, 1958, *55*, 25–30.

GOULET, L. R. New directions for research on adult retention. In D. B. Lumsden & R. H. Sherron (Eds.), *Experimental studies in adult learning and memory*. Washington, D.C.: Hemisphere Publishing, 1975.

HARLOW, H. The formation of learning sets. *Psychological Review*, 1949, *56*, 51–65.

HILGARD, E. R., & BOWER, G. H. *Theories of learning*, Fourth edition. Englewood Cliffs, New Jersey: Prentice-Hall, 1975.

HOWELL, S. C. Familiarity and complexity in perceptual recognition. In D. B. Lumsden & R. H. Sherron (Eds.), *Experimental studies in adult learning and memory*. Washington, D.C.: Hemisphere Publishing, 1975.

HULICKA, I. M. Age differences in retention as a function of interference. *Journal of Gerontology*, 1967, *22*, 180–184.

HULICKA, I. M. Aging and retention: Methodological considerations and research problems. In D. B. Lumsden & R. H. Sherron (Eds.), *Experimental studies in adult learning and memory*. Washington, D.C.: Hemisphere Publishing, 1975.

HUTCHISON, S. L. Simultaneous measurement of two types of social reinforcers in young and elderly subjects. *Dissertation Abstracts International*, 1973, *34*, 23–40.

JAMES, W. *The principles of psychology*. New York: Holt, Rinehart and Winston, 1890.

KAUSLER, D. H., & LAIR, C. V. Associative strength and paired associate learning in elderly subjects. *Journal of Gerontology*, 1966, *21*, 278–280.

KAUSLER, D. H., & LAIR, C. V. Informative feedback conditions and verbal discrimination learning in elderly subjects. *Psychonomic Science*, 1968, *10*, 193–194.

KAY, H. Theories of learning and aging. In J. E. Birren (Ed.), *Handbook of aging and the individual: Psychological and biological aspects*. Chicago: University of Chicago Press, 1967.

KIMBLE, G. A. *Hilgard and Marquis' conditioning and learning*. Second edition. Englewood Cliffs, N. J.: Prentice-Hall, 1961.

KIMBLE, G. A., & PENNYPACKER, H. W. Eyelid conditioning in young and aged subjects. *Journal of Genetic Psychology*, 1963, *103*, 283–289.

KLING, J. W. Learning: Introductory survey. In J. W. Kling & L. A. Riggs (Eds.), *Woodworth and Schlosberg's experimental psychology*, Third edition, Volume II: Learning, motivation, and memory. New York: Holt, Rinehart, and Winston, 1972.

LAIR, C. V., & MOON, H. W. The effects of praise and reproof on performance of middle aged and older subjects. *Aging and Human Development*, 1972, *3*, 279–284.

LEECH, S. J. Expectancies of young and old adults as related to type of tasks and reinforcement schedule. *Dissertation Abstracts International*, 1974, *35*, 3023.

LEECH, S., & WITTE, K. L. Paired associate learning in elderly adults as related to pacing and incentive conditions. *Developmental Psychology*, 1971, *5*, 180.

MONGE, R. H. Learning in the adult years: Set or rigidity. *Human Development*, 1969, *12*, 131–140.

MONGE, R., & HULTSCH, D. Paired associate learning as function of adult age and length of the anticipation and inspection intervals. *Journal of Gerontology*, 1971, *26*, 157–162.

PALMORE, E. *Normal aging*. Durham, N. C.: Duke University Press, 1970.

PALMORE, E. (Ed.). *Normal aging II*. Durham, N. C.: Duke University Press, 1974.

POSTMAN, L. Studies of learning to learn, II. Changes in transfer as a function of practice.

Journal of Verbal Learning and Verbal Behavior, 1964, *3,* 437–447.

POSTMAN, L. Transfer, interference, and forgetting. In J. W. Kling & L. A. Riggs (Eds.), *Woodworth and Schlosberg's experimental psychology,* Third Edition. New York: Holt, Rinehart and Winston, 1972.

PREMACK, D. Toward empirical behavior laws, I: Positive reinforcement. *Psychological Review,* 1959, *66,* 219–233.

PREMACK, D. Reversibility of the reinforcement relation. *Science,* 1962, *136,* 255–257.

RAZRAN, G. *Mind in evolution.* Boston: Houghton Mifflin, 1971.

SHOCK, N. W. The physiology of aging. *Scientific American,* 1962, *206,* 100–110.

TAUB, H. A. Paired associates learning as a function of age, rate, and instructions. *Journal of Genetic Psychology,* 1967, *111,* 41–46.

TENBRINK, T. D., DUNATHAN, A. T., & AGRUSO, V. M. JR. Effects of external reward on paired associate learning in a group setting. *Contemporary Educational Psychology,* 1976, *1,* 207–212.

TOLMAN, E. C., & HONZIK, C. H. Introduction and removal of reward and maze performance in rats. *University of California Publications of Psychology,* 1930, *4,* 257–275.

TRAXLER, A. J., & BRITTON, J. H. Age differences in retroaction as a function of anticipation interval and transfer paradigm. *Proceedings of the 78th Annual Convention of the American Psychological Association,* 1970, *78,* 683–684.

WEINER, B. Motivational factors in short term retention, II: Rehearsal or arousal? *Psychological Reports,* 1967, *20,* 1203–1208.

WELFORD, A. T. Motivation, capacity, learning, and age. *International Journal of Aging and Human Development,* 1976, *7,* 189–199.

WILKIE, F. L., & EISDORFER, C. L. Sex, verbal ability, and pacing differences in serial learning. *Journal of Gerontology,* 1977, *12,* 63–67.

WIMER, R. E., & WIGDOR, B. T. Age differences in retention of learning. *Journal of Gerontology,* 1958, *13,* 291–295.

WINN, F. J. JR., & ELIAS, J. W. The total time principle as a substitute for the pacing variable in paired associate tasks with the aged. *Experimental Aging Research,* 1975, *1,* 307–312.

WINN, F. J. JR., ELIAS, J. W., & MARSHALL, P. H. Meaningfulness and interference as factors in paired associate learning with the aged. *Educational Gerontology: An International Quarterly,* 1976, *1,* 297–306.

WITTE, K. L. Paired associate learning in young and elderly adults as related to presentation rate. *Psychological Bulletin,* 1975, *82,* 975–985.

WITTELS, I. Age and stimulus meaningfulness in paired associate learning. *Journal of Gerontology,* 1972, *27,* 372–375.

ZARETSKY, H. H., & HALBERSTAM, J. L. Age differences in paired associate learning. *Journal of Gerontology,* 1968, *23,* 165–168. (a)

ZARETSKY, H., & HALBERSTAM, J. Effects of aging, brain damage, and associative strength on paired associate learning and relearning. *Journal of Genetic Psychology,* 1968, *112,* 149–163. (b)

3

Memory

How does the human organism store incoming stimuli and subsequently retrieve whatever has been stored in order to emit the correct or incorrect responses demanded by environmental contingencies? How is information registered and organized by a memory system in view of the interference from interaction, of an exponential nature, between incoming stimuli and neural impulses? These and similar questions have interested investigators since the time of Hermann Ebbinghaus (1850–1909), who developed a systematic approach to the experimental analysis of memory through the use of nonsense syllables, becoming the first to demonstrate that forgetting decreased as a function of rehearsal.

The importance of memory is clear, since it is almost inconceivable that an organism could learn anything without some record of past experiences. Indeed, the study of memory has dominated human learning and memory research since the middle 1950s.

The information processing model, as contrasted with S–R theory, is currently dominant in the study of human memory. I will also deal briefly with the neuro-physiological basis of memory, incorporating hypotheses from recent holographic theory; my interpretation of the models and the data generated out of them will be somewhat eclectic (notwithstanding the potential limitations) in the sense that my discussions will be from within either an S–R learning or information processing framework, as appropriate.

Initially, I will present a brief review of retention measures and an overview of memory models as introductory, background material to my treatment of experimental studies (with emphasis on the behavioral) in adult memory which directly or indirectly test hypotheses generated from these theories. Amplification of this material will occur as appropriate throughout the remaining portion of the chapter. The reader should recognize that, in my opinion, the area of learning and memory is the most scientifically rigorous in all of psychology and that the extent to which I go in my discussion of same is directly related to my (ultimate) interest in the effects of aging on one's ability to remember whatever is to be remembered.

MEASURES OF RETENTION AND FORGETTING

Earlier, a distinction was established between learning and performance in which learning was described as an inference made from observable performance parameters. Similarly, investigators construe a distinction between learning and memory; however, the two processes are inextricably related to the degree that it becomes extraordinarily difficult to render them functionally distinct. Learning, for example, is related to the acquisition of basic principles in general, whereas memory is related to the retention of phenomena occurring in time and place in particular, with both processes involving the same mechanism. Consider this: Insofar as one does not learn, one has "little to recall." Conversely, if one's memory is poor, there is no sign of one's having learned very much [Botwinick, 1973, p. 254]." One infers memory for a response if the desired response is emitted at the time of testing. Unless the organism exhibits a desired response or a predicted change in behavior, one could assume forgetting, because of a failure in performance.

This assumption, of course, is fallacious, since in this instance there are at the very minimum two possibilities that could account for the absence (unavailability) of a desired response:

1. The desired response or information was not learned initially, in which event we have a problem of learning.
2. The information is *available* but not *accessible* during the retention test, in which case we have a problem of retrieval.

Mandler (1967a) suggests that all stored information is available but that only a portion of it is accessible (i.e., is sensitive to recall) at any given time. The nature of its accessibility is a partial function of retrieval cues that may or may not be present in the recall situation.

In sum, the fundamental phenomena considered in measuring memory processes are (*a*) an input phase in which a stimulus response enters the nervous system; (*b*) a secondary phase in which whatever entered the system intitially is stored
in the form of an engram (memory trace) within the nervous system; and, finally
(*c*), an output phase in which whatever is stored is subject to retrieval in recognition or recall form. Obviously, individual investigators, no one of whom will
by himself resolve the contrary evidence found in memory research will, in ac-
cordance with their priorities, study specific, discrete aspects of these enormously complicated phases. The basic problem in learning and retention studies, however, involves the manipulation of experimental procedures and materials in
order to determine differential effects on the performance of varied age groups.

Perhaps a review of procedures for measuring memory, such as recognition,
recall, relearning, and reminiscence would be useful at this point. Indeed, they
are methodologically similar to the measurement of learning. We are all familiar
with objective-type tests in which one is to identify (recognize) the correct response among several alternatives (multiple choice) or between two choices (true–
false or yes–no). In recall, one is asked a question (e.g., essay type), the answer
to which the individual must generate from information accumulated through
experience. Also, one could be instructed to reproduce original material in the
absence of cues. In relearning, or the savings method, an individual is required to
learn material for the second time. The difference between the amount of time
or number of trials to criterion required for original learning and subsequent
learning is referred to as savings.

On a *recognition* test, the correct response is identified from among a number
of alternatives. Presumably, the correct or desired response will be recognized if
the individual learned the original relevant material, which consequently entered
a storage system. However, the correct answer is not necessarily recognized
because it was in memory but because the individual could have made a good
guess. The good guess is a partial function of the individual's having had sufficient, although incomplete, information about the correct response to make a
distinction among alternatives. Also, through the process of elimination, one can
often reject the wrong alternatives, thereby increasing the probability of guessing
the correct response from among the remaining alternatives, none of which assumes the correct response was ever in memory.

Compared to recognition, *recall* is somewhat more complex, since the individual is given a minimum of external cues from which to draw in order to make
the correct response. For example, in serial recall the individual must recall a
word in the exact one-by-one order in which it was learned. In this procedure
the person is to anticipate the word following the word just presented.

Comparatively, there is more forgetting in recall (whether the mode of presentation is serial or free recall or paired associates) than in recognition because
of interference among multiple possibilities, as opposed to the more restricted

range of alternatives in the latter method. In addition, recall seems to involve both retrieval and recognition, since once the word is retrieved through search it must also be recognized as the correct word in the correct order from among the other words in the list. In sum, recall involves both search and retrieval of stored information, while recognition apparently does not require retrieval. In the former, complete learning is essential to correct responding, whereas only partial learning is sufficient in the latter.

We are already familiar with the procedures for presenting material to experimental subjects in verbal learning and memory studies; however, I would like to mention two relatively new basic techniques used in memory tasks. Namely, the *distractor* technique in which the subject is presented material to be learned, as is usual; however, the lists to be learned are short lists, and, at designated intervals, interpolated activity is introduced to prevent rehearsal by diverting (distracting) the subject's attention from the relevant task. A distinct advantage derived from its usage is that a complete curve of forgetting is demonstrated in one experimental session. Also, there is the *probe* technique, in which the subject is presented a list of material of which only one item is relevant. For example, in a serial-recall list, the probe item is one of the items in the list and the target or test item is the one immediately following the probe item. Utilization of this technique yields a curve of memory influenced only to a slight degree by practice.

There are compound variations of the probe and distractor techniques, along with a variety of other new, sophisticated storage and retrieval instructions that elicit a recall or recognition response. For a detailed discussion, see Craik and Tulving (1975).

In the *relearning* or *savings* method, introduced by Ebbinghaus, the initial time required by the individual to learn the material is compared with the time the individual takes to relearn the original material. The amount of forgetting is a function of the time differences in relearning the original material (i.e., of how much time is saved in relearning). If, however, no forgetting occurs, perfect performance is observed on the first relearning trial. Savings will vary as a function of the amount of forgetting or retention of the originally learned material.

The savings method grew out of Ebbinghaus's early investigations dealing with the relationship of nonsense syllables to meaningful material. While in his thirties he memorized stanzas of *Don Juan*. Later, in his fifties, after over 20 years of not having seen them, he relearned them. Despite his observation that he had completely forgotten them, he exhibited savings in the time taken to relearn the stanzas (Hilgard, 1964). Thus, in the absence of recognition or recall, it would appear that partial effects of initial learning are retained.

Finally, reminiscence is an aspect of memory in which a subject is simply asked to reflect on past experience and to recall whatever is relevant to the subject or to the investigator. Havighurst (1972) defines it as either intentional thinking back in an attempt to recall and reconstruct experiences or just letting thoughts flow spontaneously. Typically, one would not be asked to recall facts in order to make a decision. In either event, there is the problem of accuracy of recollection, since the investigator must rely on the individual's report of the "truth" in the absence of an objective measure of validity. Questionnaires have been developed to test its reliability; however, from an empirical point of view, these would seem to be questionable.

The value of this form of recall as an aspect of memory seems to lie in its relationship to one's overall adaptive behavior, since it appears to be a universal phenomenon, in varying degrees, after about age 10 or so.

MEMORY MODELS

It was out of the Ebbinghaus method of varying retention intervals in verbal-learning studies that later investigators replicated and expanded his technique to provide evidence for a short-term retention of verbal items, which implied that memory had a compound nature. Specifically, Brown (1958) and Peterson and Peterson (1959) demonstrated that forgetting of nonsense syllables was remarkable after a few seconds' time span. On the other hand, Sperling (1960) called attention to a primary sensory storage system, thereby relegating short-term storage to a secondary position, since all incoming stimuli must enter through the senses. His investigations indicated that verbal material lasted in the visual system for about 200 milliseconds if the material were not processed further. Thus, Sperling's findings suggest at least three stages in memory. The first is a complete trace of stimuli impinging on the organism in the sensory system. The second is short-term memory (STM), out of which one immediately recalls material before it decays. The third is long-term memory (LTM) of a relatively permanent nature, which contains material that has been learned. To account for the multiplicity of stages in the memory process, investigators began theorizing on the nature of information processing in the human. The dominant model, using the computer analogy and having three stores (sensory, short term, and long term) was that of Atkinson and Shiffrin (1968), to which we now turn.

Human Information Processing

Similar to a computer, human memory can be construed as characterized by input–output operations, with limitations defined by the nature of a program's instructions.

Atkinson and Shiffrin (1968) suggest that information is transferred from STM to LTM to become a fixed feature of memory. "The important aspect of this transfer, however, is the wide variance in the amount and form of the transferred information that may be induced by control processes [Atkinson & Shiffrin, 1968, p. 106]."

Control processes, as one aspect of processing, refer to the strategies an individual will use in handling information. Control of rehearsal is one such strategy used by an individual, contingent upon experimental conditions and individual differences. It is construed as a temporary feature (lending itself well to modification) of memory, whereas the *ability* to rehearse is a fixed structural feature, a second aspect of processing, having a neurological base (not modifiable). Short- and long-term memory are also permanent features.) In sum, the decisions to select out specific aspects of an information pool, whether or not to rehearse them, and when to retrieve the information are under the voluntary control of the individual and are called "control processes" in memory.

If the individual directs attention to the rehearsal strategy (control process), then the transferred information is relatively weak and sensitive to interference effects. If, on the other hand, attention is focused on coding operations (control process), then that information increases in strength. Atkinson and Shiffrin refer to the coding process as a modification (and therefore change) of information in STM as a function of the search (control process) operations of LTM.

At this point I caution the reader of the danger of oversimplification in summarizing enormously complicated theories of memory; however, as stated earlier, my purpose is to treat those aspects of learning and memory that are amenable to experimental analyses on the effects of aging as such. I am therefore not particularly interested in the broad theoretical implications of highly complex memory structures that may or may not be testable or, more importantly, may not be applicable to the educational gerontology area.

At any rate, in synoptic form, the Atkinson–Shiffrin model posits that information is processed through three identifiable storage systems: (*a*) a sensory register in which incoming stimuli are held temporarily and are subject to decay and interference effects from additional incoming stimuli; (*b*) an STM of variable capacity in which a limited amount of information can be processed contingent upon one's memory span, which is a function of information decay in STM and of rehearsal that increases the strength of decaying information; and (*c*) LTM, in which learned material is of a relatively permanent form but, nonetheless, is also subject to decay and loss of accessibility through interference, as observed in the retrieval process when one initiates a search strategy.

Some investigators have proposed alternatives to the computer metaphor and to the stage (STM and LTM) model of memory, of which one is referred to as the "levels of processing" construct.

Levels of Processing

In contrast to the computer model of Atkinson and Shiffrin, Craik and Lockhart (1972) propose a "levels of processing" framework that suggests that the real issue in memory research is the nature of the processing that the material to-be-remembered has undergone. They submit that as depth of processing increases, forgetting decreases. The initial level refers to the processing of physical properties of incoming stimuli. The following level is deeper than the first and refers to the recognition or discrimination of the incoming stimuli as discrete, whereas the next deeper level refers to input that is organized as a function of its meaningful aspects. Expressed differently, perfunctory processing results in an STM condition, whereas deep processing leads to an LTM condition.

It was Craik and Lockhart's dissatisfaction with a multistorage or "box" approach to memory research that led to their formulation of a levels of processing framework, which, they felt, was also subject to modification through additional research resulting from well-designed questions. Their specific criticism of previous models related to their marked limitations in explaining the capacity, coding, and forgetting aspects of memory. In order to obviate contrary evidence of these phenomena, one approach is to direct attention to the encoding operations themselves and to entertain the notion that rates of forgetting are directly related to the nature of encoding.

According to these investigators, memory lies along a continuum from the temporary, limited traces of sensory interpretations to the more permanent traces of meaningful associations. Memory is related to perceptual processing levels that may or may not be categorized into stages such as sensory interpretation and pattern recognition. Processing levels may be more useful if conceptualized as a continuum of analysis.

The levels of processing construct involves a central processor mechanism which can be directed to any level of processing. To the extent that items are in the processor and are therefore receiving attention, they are not subject to forgetting. However, if the processor is diverted from these items, the rate of forgetting becomes a function of the level of processing for the items; that is, the material is lost at a rate defined by its level of processing, so that rates of forgetting are slower for the deeper levels.

By way of summary, Craik and Lockhart suggest that the memory trace is a function of perceptual processing, in the sense that perception can be construed as a pattern of interpretations. These analyses begin at the sensory level and proceed to semantic–associative operations, so that the nature of the memory trace is related to the extent of perceptual analysis of the stimulus. The strength of a trace corresponds to the level of processing, so that items receiving full attention and analysis with associations (i.e., deep analysis and processing) lead to relatively permanent traces, while items receiving less than full attention lead to temporary (transient) traces.

Finally, they focus on Type I rehearsal, which refers to the continued processing of items already analyzed solely in order to maintain their accessibility, and Type II rehearsal, which involves a deeper analysis of items that leads to improved memory under retrieval conditions.

DISCUSSION

There is conflicting evidence as to whether all verbal material is stored in a unitary system or whether there are different types of memories corresponding to the nature of input and, moreover, to the kind of operation performed on that input. Let us therefore examine some of the arguments surrounding the issues.

Depth of Processing

Craik and Tulving (1975) review some of the advantages of the levels framework, such as its emphasis on the dynamics of trace formation and encoding (input) operations and its obviation of the necessity to verify limits of storage capacity in order to specify the coding characteristic of each level or to describe the transfer of material from one level to another as a function of a specific mechanism. However, despite the advantages, the approach has some limitations. These researchers therefore have raised the following question: Does the levels of processing framework say anything more than that meaningful events are well remembered?

The most obvious shortcoming of this notion is that rate of forgetting is not functionally distinct on an invariant basis and therefore is not predictable. There is thus a sort of circularity present in the framework, since rate of forgetting is a function of level of processing, but depth of processing is defined after rate of forgetting has been defined.

Craik and Tulving (1975) described 10 experiments conducted within the levels framework, and although one basic paradigm was used throughout the investigations, they utilized several variations, the discussion of which is beyond the scope of this chapter. Briefly, subjects were informed that they were participating in a perception and speed of reaction study in which they would be presented words over a number of trials. Prior to presentation of the word, each subject was given a question which was to initiate processing of the word to various levels of analysis. Processing to a shallow level involved questions about the physical properties of the word, whereas processing to a deeper level involved questions related to the meaning of the word. For example, typical questions such as "Is the word an animal name?" and "Would the word fit the following sentence?" were asked. Subjects would then answer yes or no. Following the question and answer trials, subjects were given an unexpected free recall or recognition test covering the words used in the initial phase of the study. The general hypothesis was that deeper level questions would result in a more sophisticated memory trace, which in turn would be related to higher performance scores.

I would like to mention, in addition, that the incidental learning paradigm, a model which lends itself well to testing the levels notion, was used in at least three of the experiments reported, since it seems entirely appropriate to conceptualize incidental learning as a shallower level of processing than intentional learning, in which one has focused attention on the material to be learned. (The reader is reminded that instructions for intentional learning relate directly to what is expected of the subject, whereas for incidental learning the instructions relate to performance on a task other than the one on which the subject is tested, so that the test material has received only partial attention. I am not suggesting that the underlying mechanism is different in these operationally defined kinds of learning.)

These investigators concluded that recall or recognition of words is a function of the nature of the encoding operations carried out on the items, contrary to earlier evidence, which placed emphasis on such phenomena as intention to learn, degree of effort, task difficulty, decision times, extent of rehearsal, etc. They point out that traditional paradigms described memory traces and associations in terms of strength. Acquisition, retention, transfer, and retrieval were in turn a function of strength of associations. In the present series of experiments, however, the traditional determinants of strength were held constant. The independent variable was the mental activity of the learner, as influenced to varying degrees through instructions, for example and thus it was shown to be a significant factor in memory performance. The authors submit that subjects do not remember what was "out there," but what they *did* during encoding.

The results of their experiments indicate that presentation of "learn" instructions is not related to the best performance. Rather, when learners are presented with material along with instructions to learn, they use idiosyncratic encoding operations on the material to be learned.

Short-Term Memory

In our everyday discussions we often refer to those events or aspects of experience that we tend to forget in one instance or to remember in another, which suggests that memory functions in at least two different manners; that is, on short-term and long-term bases. On the one hand, we recall telephone numbers up to several minutes after the first exposure and then forget them, which for some serves as an example of STM. If, on the other hand, the number is a frequently used one, the continued repetition or rehearsal of that number is related to its entrance into LTM, where it has the potential of being recalled at a later time without reference to the telephone directory (i.e., the number has been learned and therefore committed to LTM in a relatively permanent form).

Thus, the processing of information into LTM apparently demands that it remain in STM for ample processing time, which is subject to interference from competing events, such as interpolated activity.

To illustrate the phenomena of proactive and retroactive interference, Peterson and Peterson (1959) conducted an STM study in which subjects were asked to recall a consonant–vowel–consonant (CVC) trigram after varying retention intervals of 3–18 seconds before recall. During the retention intervals subjects counted backward by threes or fours to prevent rehearsal until a light signaled for them to recall the trigram. This distraction task was both unimportant to the memory task itself and cumbersome. The investigators found that as retention interval increased, accuracy of recall decreased to the extent that after 18 seconds accuracy was reduced to virtually nothing (despite the fact that recall of three letters is relatively simple).

The interpolated activity apparently served as interference to the correct recall of the trigram, the possibility of decay during the time interval notwithstanding. These investigators interpreted their findings as favorable to the passive decay (as a mechanism of forgetting) hypothesis. For our purposes, the study is important because it demonstrates rapid forgetting, which defines STM as distinct from LTM, where material is retained for longer periods of time. Subsequent to this study, an enormous amount of research has been conducted on the duplex theory of memory.

Serial Position Effects

McGeoch and Irion (1952) report that since the early studies recounted by Ebbinghaus in the 1870s investigators have found that when one memorizes a list of nonsense or meaningful materials one learns the beginning (primacy) and the end (recency) more readily than the middle portion. If the absolute number of errors made at each position of the list is plotted, a serial position curve invariably results; that is, a curve showing bowness and skewness in which beginning items have the least errors, middle items the most, and those at the end the next least number of errors appears. Glanzer and Cunitz (1966) suggested that recency represents items in STM and conducted a test of the hypothesis that the serial position curve is a function of output from short- and long-term storage mechanisms. They submitted that recall of material from the primacy end is output from LTM, whereas recall of material from the recency position is output from STM, thereby providing the research community with a vehicle to produce evidence for a multistore memory.

At any rate, the relative invariance of position effects (on serial position curves) in rote verbal learning has been demonstrated under many conditions in which a wide variety of stimulus materials were used. Various theories have been submitted that presumably account for the serial position effect, although until 1952 the Lepley–Hull theory had received the most support, either through empirical evidence or theoretical analysis. This theory essentially posits that the serial position curve is a functon of the degree of inhibition associated with responses to the middle segment of the list (intralist interference). A number of experiments conducted to test this theory and several other hypotheses yield data that indicate that the shape (bowness and skewness) of the curve is invariant under a wide range of experimental procedures and conditions, such as massed and distributed practice, instructions, association strength of items, variations in retention and interitem intervals, length of list, and "differences in learning ability and extraexperimental conditions beyond formal retroactive and proactive inhibition [Agruso & Reckase, 1976, p. 569]."

The interference theory of memory accounts for the position effect in terms of bonds or associations of items within the list to be learned. Expressed differently, learning is considered to be the formation of new associations between each item of the list with every other item of the list; that is, it follows the laws of conditioning and is therefore subject to extinction and spontaneous recovery. End items are easier to learn than middle items because of less competition or interference by adjacent items.

Information processing theory, on the other hand, suggests that a learner processes one item at a time until the item is committed to memory. Just as a computer encodes, stores, operates upon, and retrieves information, so does the human organism, through the central nervous system. This approach construes learning the list to be a function of the learner's particular perceptual (attention) strategy. Studies generated by these accounts of the serial position effect provide experimental evidence for short- and long-term storage in the memory process.

Murdock (1960), in response to the paradoxical experimental findings with respect to the serial position curve, stated that "it would almost seem that the shape of the serial position curve has nothing whatsoever to do with learning . . . since it seems to be unaffected by variables that are known to affect rate of learning [p. 24]." Murdock submits that the curve is due to the unequal distinctiveness of the items because of their ordinal position within the list; that is, initial items are more distinctive than middle items.

In view of the foregoing, it would seem appropriate to go beyond the learning variables. If the curve is not a function of learning, then perhaps it is a function of developmental level (age). Directly related to this, Agruso and Reckase (1976) conducted a verbal-learning study to determine if the curve remains invariant across developmental age levels under different rote learning tasks when the curves are expressed as Indices of Relative Difficulty (transformed error scores).

Eighty students, aged 5 through 11, served as subjects for their study. Each subject participated in two experimental tasks, multitrial free recall and serial recall. Seven words for each of the tasks constituted the list length. A multiple discriminant analysis on the transformed error scores of the four age levels indicates "that age or grade level in and of itself is not a significant factor in changing the bowed skewed curve found in rote verbal learning tasks [p. 569]."

Expressed differently, there were no significant differences in performance of the developmental levels studied in terms of mean indices of relative difficulty at each position (Agruso & Reckase, 1976).

In addition, and perhaps more pertinent at this point, is the fact that the effect of position on the curve was found to be consistent with findings reported by other researchers. The serial position effect demands explanation by any model of memory, since the same effect is observed in STM and LTM studies, the same kind of proactive inhibition and rates of forgetting as a function of item similarity, all of which could be interpreted as evidence for one memory characterized by different modes of expression.

Long-Term Memory

The notion of a dual memory process was first systematically investigated by D. O. Hebb (1949), who described memory processes in terms of neuronal changes, which, of course, is clearly a physiological theory, notwithstanding his behavioristic tendencies. For Hebb (1972), STM is a "reverberation in the closed loops of the cell assembly and between cell assemblies while LTM is more structural, a lasting change of synaptic connections [p. 97]." The hypothetical dual process operates together. Long-term memory is seen as a function of the amount of time the reverberation of STM lasts.

In other words, Hebb suggests that a network of neuronal activity repeatedly exciting each other is the basis for STM, while structural changes in the neuronal network form the basis for LTM. For him, memory is the retention of learning, viewed as a permanent modification of transmission pathways. Memories are stored throughout cortical areas of the brain and not in a single neuron.

To illustrate a dual process in memory storage, Hebb (1961, pp. 37–51) conducted a study on the effects of repetition on memory. College students were instructed to repeat, in the exact order of presentation, a series of nine digits, which were read to them at a rate of one digit per second over 24 trials. The same nine digits were used on each trial but were given in random orders. Every third series was identical; however, the students were unaware of that. Results indicated consistent improvement with rehearsal of the repeated digits and stabilized performance for the randomized series of digits. Both short-term and long-term retention increments are observed when the material to be recalled is repeated before the retention test. Hebb pointed out that if there is a distinction between LTM and STM, recall of both sequences should be similar; however, as indicated, repetition increased performance (which, of course, is contrary to his initial position).

Hebb suggests that the repetition every third trial had an additive effect on the storage of that material. In other words, the STM of nine digits, even after careful attention, is temporary. The listening of the next series of digits interferes with the recall of the following series; however, and more importantly, there is apparently some trace or beginning of structural change. What is erased through interference is STM; however, the trace (through repetition) after each third trial forms the basis of LTM, which is relatively permanent. However, its permanency is a function of interference patterns that may or may not affect what has been stored. In other words, a consolidation period (15–60 minutes) in which stored material remains undisturbed is demanded by LTM.

Melton (1963) replicated the Hebb experiment, reporting similar results. He suggested that both immediate and delayed recall are affected similarly by task conditions. Thus, the existence of distinct memory mechanisms is questionable, and it could be that STM and LTM lie along a continuum. Given that a distinction between STM and LTM is by no means clear at this point, the Hebb and Melton results have been interpreted as evidence for independent and parallel processes; that is, the digits listened to entered STM and LTM concurrently. (It would seem that the real problem in LTM is that of the retrieval process.)

Waugh and Norman (1965) pointed out that investigators had fallaciously assumed that items held for several seconds must be retrieved from STM. They suggested, however, that items could enter LTM quickly, while at the same time remaining in STM. Thus, recall of items is a function of STM *and* LTM processes.

These investigators would utilize the notion of two stages in memory, but, rather than defining them in terms of the task or retention interval, they would use the concepts of "primary memory" (PM) and "secondary memory" (SM), both of which refer to STM. The ambiguities concerning the theoretical relationships between PM and SM to LTM are beyond the scope of this book. Items in PM are maintained through the process of rehearsal through which items are transferred to SM. Specifically, up to four items are temporarily *held* and *organized* in PM as processing for permanent registration (and retrieval) in SM.

At any rate, if one assumes two kinds of storage, then the nature of the distinction is that STM is of limited capacity while LTM is virtually unlimited; that is, viewed from a physiological framework, there are 10–12 billion neurons in the brain, the interconnections of which have the potential for storing a practically infinite amount of information. In addition, RNA molecules are also capable of storing great quantities of information, which is discussed on p. 72.

Let us now turn to the brain structures required for the storage and retrieval of information.

NEUROLOGICAL CORRELATES OF MEMORY

There is little doubt that the human organism's nervous structure is changed with each new experience, a change that is somehow registered by the nervous system for a relatively permanent period of time.

One approach to the study of brain and behavior demonstrates that the CNS is capable of modifying incoming sensory stimuli. From this frame of reference interest lies in how information is transformed and coded. Another approach is to study how incoming stimuli modify (change) the CNS so that the change can influence future information processing.

There are a variety of techniques within the physiological psychology paradigm that attempt to gain evidence to the specific mechanisms utilized in the acquisition, retention, and retrieval of information and in brain changes; however, I shall discuss briefly the findings of the brain lesion technique, omitting the electrophysiological approach. In a later section I shall deal with the chemical approach to the investigation of memory, in which a chemical agent is administered to subjects, whose behavioral (or molecular) changes are then observed.

The real problem, however, concerns the organism's ability to adapt to a changing environment. As discussed earlier, the nature of the phenomena observed in learning and memory (including retrieval) is contingent upon the state of the organism's entire system.

Anatomical Aspects

Studies by Rosenzweig, Bennett, and Diamond (1972) have demonstrated that experience does produce observable anatomical and chemical changes in the brains of rats. They found that the level of acetylcholinesterase in the brain was changed by problem-solving tasks and that additional new experiences changed the weight of the rat's brain. (As indicated earlier, the explanation of the relationship of these changes to learning and memory will come from cross-disciplinary research.)

In a series of further studies on the effects of an enriched versus an impoverished environment, Rosenzweig et al. (1972) reported that rats from each environment differed in such a way that

> rats with an enriched experience had a greater weight of cerebral cortex, a
> greater thickness of cortex and a greater total activity of acetylcholinesterase
> but less activity of the enzyme per unit of tissue weight. Moreover, . . . consid-
> erably greater activity of another enzyme: cholinesterase, which is found in
> the glial cells and blood capillaries that surround the nerve cells . . . more glial
> cells . . . which may account for the increased activity of cholinesterase. . . .
> The greatest differences . . . were found in the occipital cortex, which is rough-
> ly the rear third of the cortical surface [p. 24].

Thus, the evidence of changes in the brain as a function of experience is compelling; however, its importance is not that it provides direct evidence for memory storage but that it demonstrates the brain's sensitivity to environmental stimuli, which of course is essential to a physiological theory of memory. Some questions that baffled investigators even before the early investigation of Karl

Lashley have not been resolved. For instance: How are brain cells changed by experience, and what are the functions of brain structures in the process of the storing of information? What are the necessary and sufficient conditions to effect alterations in the nervous system so that *traces* have the potential to affect behavior following the initial input? Deutsch (1969) provides a detailed discussion of these and similar questions related to the physiological basis for learning and memory. He also includes sources on RNA transfer phenomena.

The Engram

An additional question remains unanswered: Where is the locus of what has been learned; that is, where is memory recording past experience stored in the brain? Karl Lashley (1960) once remarked, "I sometimes feel, in reviewing the evidence on the localization of the memory trace, that the necessary conclusion is that learning just is not possible. Nevertheless, in spite of such evidence against it, learning does sometimes occur [p. 501]."

For over 30 years, Lashley searched for the locus of the memory trace (engram). In 1950 he reported that a cortical localization of the engram had not been found. The method used by Lashley was to condition animals on acquisition and retention tasks and then to produce lesions (cortical destruction) in specific regions of the cortex. Although brain lesions have been observed to disrupt the retention of some tasks (simple visual learning, for example), Lashley was looking for specific regions (assuming that the brain is divided into a system of discrete units, each with a specific role) where ablation would neutralize an engram. Apparently, the engram was not totally removed. Rather, a neural pathway to the memory trace was destroyed, thereby making accessibility to the memory difficult.

He submitted that his extensive research failed to produce evidence of a specific location in the brain for the memory trace because engrams were stored in diverse places throughout the brain's cortical and subcortical areas.

Although he failed to destroy specific long-term memories, he derived the law of mass action, which essentially states that disruption of memory is an increasing function of the amount of tissue destroyed; that is, the more the tissue damage, the more it affects one's behavior. Some additional general conclusions are that new associations are inextricably related and connected to similar associations and that the cells of the brain are in a state of constant activity, so that, in an instance of reproductive memory, recall involves millions of neurons to the extent that the same neurons holding memory traces of one event are also involved in an immense amount of other activity. Finally, learning and retention involves a complex of neurons which change and thereby subsequently become sensitive to a specific stimulus or pattern of stimuli as a function of unknown mechanisms.

Cortical Stimulation

The neurosurgeon Wilder Penfield (1954) reports that memories have been evoked by electrical stimulation of the temporal lobe of human patients scheduled for brain surgery. A selected area of exposed temporal cortex was electrically stimulated, and patients were asked to report their immediate response. Past experience in the form of vivid visual images or the vivid hearing of specific sounds was reported. The recollections apparently included all the details associated with the original experience, including the original emotional reactions.

Subsequent electrical stimulation of the exact cortical area which was mapped following the initial stimulation produced the same reports too at different times. In other words, the stimulus apparently directly evoked a precise memory. In Penfield's words (1969):

> A stimulating electrode, applied to the surface of the interpretive cortex of a conscious man, sometimes selects a moment in past time and causes the stream of consciousness to flow again. This record apparently includes all that the individual was aware of at the time, things seen and heard in normal detail, things felt and believed. The flashback strips of experience, which have been summoned thus from the past, include . . . all of the individual's awareness and nothing of what he ignored.
>
>   It is clear that the neuronal action that accompanies each succeeding state of consciousness leaves its permanent imprint on the brain. The imprint, or record, is a trail of facilitation of neuronal connections that can be followed again by an electronic current many years later with no loss of detail, as though a tape recorder had been receiving it all [p. 165].

Significant also is the fact that when Penfield delivered the same mild electrical stimulus to other regions of the cortex, different experiences or no past experiences at all were reported by his patients. Although the experiences are reported as if they are recalled exactly as they originally happened, objective verification is lacking. The question of the extent to which distortion of the actual experience operates is unanswered. In addition, the loss of brain cells (about 20% of which are irretrievably lost by age 65 or so) over time must certainly exert some influence on the qualitative and quantitative nature of recall.

In short, researchers have traced nerve pathways in the brain through the application of mild electrical stimulation in both humans and animals. As a result of their investigations, specific areas of the cerebral cortex have been associated as visual, motor, or auditory regions.

The memory trace has not been found, however, in spite of the fact that, from a stimulus–response standpoint, nerve pathways have been established. Research findings are still at variance with the evidence of Lashley, who had demonstrated earlier that rats could still respond to pattern stimuli and perform complex learning tasks subsequent to the destruction of 80% or more of visual cortex and major nerve pathways to their brains.

The Hologram Analogy[1]

Karl Pribram and Karl Lashley have demonstrated independently that massive insult of brain tissue does not cause recognition, which is a function of memory storage, to cease. A variety of experiments dealing with persons who have suffered strokes, thereby sustaining partial destruction of a neural system, have shown that these individuals are capable both of learning new tasks and of recalling past experiences from memory. These findings provide compelling evidence that the neural circuitry essential to recognition and recall processes is distributed throughout regions within related brain networks.

Many researchers have therefore reached a consensus that whatever is stored in the brain's cortex is not only highly resistant to forgetting but is also apparently divided over large areas of brain tissue.

Karl Pribram (1969, 1972) suggests the principle of the hologram as a highly sophisticated hypothesis of information storage and suggests the analogy of a hologram as the hypothetical neural substrate of memory or as the mechanism "by which experience can be experienced [Pribram, 1969, p. 198]."

A major assumption on which the hologram analogy rests is that, initially, perception involves some neural change which is eventually recorded permanently within a neural system. What is recorded, therefore, must have properties enabling the record to be manifested, upon reception of an appropriate stimulus, in recognition or recall form. The neural hologram presumably has the properties required for an information storage system. And, in addition, it qualifiably accounts for the distributed memory mechanism in brain tissue, which can conceivably explain the failure of researchers to destroy specific memories.

Pribram, Nuwer, and Baron (1974) delineated the heuristic value of a holographic model of memory. The advantages of such a model are:

---

[1]The Pribram references explain the nature of holograms and provide explanations of the neurophysiological processes leading up to and including the making of a hologram. In addition there is discussed there the fundamental relevance of neurochemical research findings to education.

I attended a symposium, "Fourier Analysis in the Visual System and the Neural Hologram," held at Stanford University in January, 1975, in which some participants suggested that the analogy is both highly speculative and possibly nontestable. Several participants feel that the hypothesis is too simple, not only in view of the demands made by an enormously complex brain, but also because the nature of memory must be explained by factors beyond the law of mass action.

An additonal limitation lies in the fact that with the analogy Pribram is referring to *waves* and not to neural *impulses* in the brain. Since the two must interact, we are left with the enormously complex problem of interaction, with its inherent difficulty in explaining differential functions and specific contributions not only to what is stored, but to the process of storage itself.

According to some researchers the holographic model is not a theory of perception, since, among other reasons, it does not predict an individual's ability to perceive change.

Property of distributed storage: Holographic memories show large capacities, parallel processing, . . . associative storage for perceptual completion and for associative recall. The holographic hypothesis serves therefore not only as a guide to neurophysiological experiment, but also as a possible explanatory tool in understanding the mechanisms involved in behaviorally derived problems in the study of memory and perception [p. 454].

I feel that the evaluation of the holographic hypothesis is premature, since it has not been applied to a sufficient number of problems in memory. And although there remain deep ambiguities in psychological theory when principles of holography are applied to account for the structure of memory, the hypothesis is nonetheless testable and worthy of further research.

Biochemical Basis

The real problem in the study of memory from within the biochemical framework is to determine the mechanism that stores the organism's experience. Some investigators hypothesized that memories might be stored in a chemically coded state in the nucleic acids of nerve cells, namely deoxyribonucleic acid (DNA). This appeared entirely possible, since the potentially almost infinite number of various molecular patterns of DNA would explain the seemingly unlimited capacity of the brain to store experiences. Some investigators had suggested that memories were stored in ribonucleic acid (RNA); however, since this particular molecule undergoes change in some intracellular processes, its long-term storage capacity is doubtful.

The biochemical explanation suggests that an increase in activity in nerve cells is related to an increase of these cells' RNA, which is essential to the process of protein synthesis in the cells. The argument follows these lines: If the assumption is correct that there exists a bond between contiguous, repeated incoming stimuli activity and RNA, it is possible that the proteins in nerve cells function as memory traces. (I had discussed earlier the role of repetition in memory processes, suggested by many investigators as essential to permanent storage.)

Whether or not the DNA–RNA complex serves as the memory molecule is questionable. The precise role of the nucleic acids in coding and cell processes within a learning and memory context is ambiguous, to say the least.

Enesco (1967) published a review and evaluation of RNA as the memory molecule. In short, he submitted that yeast RNA is "not incorporated into brain tissue and does not increase brain synthetic activity [p. 33]." Previously, some investigators reported beneficial effects from introduction of yeast RNA into senile patients and animals; however, according to Enesco, these effects are not explained "in direct relation to the hypothesis that RNA within the brain encodes memory information [p. 33]."

ADULT MEMORY

There is a substantial body of evidence that establishes the existence of performance decrement with age in certain aspects of the memory process. Memory has been construed as a time-based process operating in the sequence sensory registration, immediate, short-term, intermediate, and long-term memories. Other concepts found in the literature are those of very short-term, preperceptual trace, stimulus trace, primary-, and secondary memory. In addition, the recent literature reflects usage of such terms as acoustic, semantic, and episodic memory, since these presumably provide the specificity implied in the usage of some of the older terms. In any case, I shall view memory as a dichotomized, time-related process (with points of emphasis alternating among processes, tasks, and retention intervals), notwithstanding the unresolved issue of whether or not there is more than one mechanism in memory.

Investigators have referred to losses in memory as stemming from deficits in either registration, storage, or retrieval. And although we will discuss registration, the emphasis will be on storage and retrieval, since these phenomena are considered the most problematic for the aged. Acquisition and retention as related to time between learning trials operationally define the particular phase of memory under study.

Learning and Memory

I will follow through here on my earlier discussion of the distinction between learning and memory, in which I suggested that they are inextricably intertwined. The usefulness of conceptualizing such a distinction comes to light when an investigator must interpret whether the aged's performance in a recall or recognition task is related to a learning or to a memory deficit. From an experimental viewpoint, it is one thing to say that the performance decrements found in the aged are a function of memory deficits; but it is not entirely out of the question that their relatively poor retention is due to a learning disability.

The evidence is compelling that the performance of the aged on learning tasks is characterized by decrements (Gladis & Braun, 1958; Jerome, 1959). On the other hand, Wimer and Wigdor (1958) found that when two age groups initially learned paired associate material equally (i.e., to criterion of one perfect repetition) no age differences in recall were observed. Jerome (1959) suggested that the elderly may recall less on delayed (memory) tests because they may have learned less during the acquisition trials. Hulicka and Weiss (1965) reported similar findings, which suggests that age related decrements are a function of degree of acquisition; that is, memory performance is related to degree of initial learning. Gilbert (1941) reported significant age differences in memory span tests, consistent with Wechsler (1944), who submitted that memory declines rapidly with age. Hulicka (1966) suggested that the subtests of the Wechsler Memory Scale may be more a measure of learning than of memory. Kriauciunas (1968) submits that, despite the ambiguities here, age differences in memory span or other forms of recall are negligible when degree of acquisition or learning is equal.

Moenster (1972) conducted a study to determine if the reported decrements in learning ability with age are due to learning or memory variables. The subjects were 192 females aged 20–94. They were divided into five age groups of 20–29, 30–39, 40–54, 55–69, and 70–94 years. Each subject was given a meaningful story of several paragraphs in length to read. *Immediately* following the reading, each subject completed a 20-item multiple-choice test which served as the measure of *learning*. Following 10 minutes of either related or unrelated interpolated tasks, subjects were given the same 20-question test which served as a measure of *memory*.

Results show that the age effect alone was significant for learning and memory ($p < .001$). However, adjustments were computed for learning scores under the memory test conditions, and age differences were not observed. Moenster interprets these findings as supportive of Jerome's (1959) conclusion, that is, that memory performance decrements are a function of learning deficits with age.

Primary and Secondary Memory

Talland (1965) designed a study to determine the effects of three sources of interference on immediate memory span. In this experiment, 200 male subjects of age range 20–69 were divided into five groups of 10 years' age span each. The three sources of interference were (a) free recall, in which the subject was instructed to recall words in any order; (b) selective recall, for which the subject was to report the unrepeated word (there is no response interference, but search and matching of items in store is essential); and (c) restrictive recall, in which all the words were to be reported in any order, but the unrepeated word was to be reported last in the list to be recalled. Lists of words ranged in length from 4 to 13 words, with varied lists of 4 to 7 words. The lists were constructed of unrelated words, with the exception of 1 word which was unrepeated, but in a different order, in each list. All words appeared twice except for the 1 unrepeated word. Results indicate that for all the lists of 4, 5, 6, or 7 words there were no significant age differences observed. However, differences were observed when lists exceeded 7 items, to the extent that, as age increased, recall decreased. This finding could be due to additional response interference from the additional items. Interference effects due to recall were not indicated until age 50. At all age levels some forgetting was found in the free-recall condition, which requires minimal organization of the word list for registration. Talland suggests that interference here is a function of the recall process itself and is beyond the immediate memory span. Decrements in selective recall are due to search and matching strategies and any subvocal recital used in a particular individual strategy. These findings have been interpreted to mean that age decrements in immediate memory result from response interference in interaction with search and matching operations, which is consistent with Talland's (1968) findings from a series of short-term retention studies in which he suggested that performance deficits in the aged that differentiate them from the young are essentially a function of an increased susceptibility to response interference. The age-related decrements in the restrictive recall condition could be related to the aged's difficulty in reorganizing verbal material.

Craik (1968) conducted a series of experiments to determine the effects of varying the length of lists on memory span in the aged and to determine the relationships of search and retrieval operations to a two store model of memory. Experiments I and II indicated a coding deficit in the older subjects, which led the author to submit that this deficit is related to registration decrements in the elderly. Experiment III showed that the older subjects required more time and trials to report letters of a brief sentence. Craik suggested that this finding could reflect retrieval problems for the older groups. Experiment IV was a test of supraspan interference; the author hypothesized that the older subjects' performance would show more decrement than a younger group's. Although the results of Talland (1965) indicated this, Craik's results were not supportive of his hypothesis. The results of Experiment V confirmed his hypothesis of deficits in retrieval with age.

Influenced by the evidence of these and other experimental findings, Craik (1968) submitted that immediate recall is characterized by a primary memory (PM) of limited capacity and a secondary memory (SM) of a larger capacity, a position similar to that of Waugh and Norman (1965). Retrieval from PM is by direct readout of existing traces, whereas retrieval from SM involves search operations. Craik suggested that PM is relatively stable over the years but that there are age related deficits in registration into and retrieval from SM.

It should be pointed out here that, in a test of his retrieval hypothesis, Craik (1968) discussed two aspects of the tasks used in experimentation, the length of the list and the scope of possible responses. As the number of items to be recalled and the scope of possible items increases, the difficulty of the task increases. The literature does indeed reflect age related deficits with difficult material (Hultsh, 1971a).

Processing Depth Hypothesis

A number of investigators have reported that the elderly have comparatively more difficulty in retention of material to be remembered if it involves a "chunking" strategy (Craik, 1968; Craik & Masani, 1967, 1969) or otherwise requires the organization of verbal material into complex, higher order units. Specifically,

an age related decrement in number of chunks (in this case, a chunk is a number
of words recalled in the exact order presented) recalled has been reported. Earlier I discussed the levels of processing model of memory, which suggested that,
as depth of processing increases, so does retention. It is hypothesized that the
elderly are unable to process verbal materials to the depth of younger subjects.
This is referred to as the "processing-deficit hypothesis"; it was tested by Hyde
and Jenkins (1973) and by Eysenck (1974), who utilized the incidental learning
paradigm in which subjects were given orienting tasks but were unaware that
they would later be tested (by recall) on the words in the tasks. The hypothesis
predicts that age related decrements should increase in extent as the depth of
processing required by the orienting task increases.

The subjects were divided into two groups of 18-30 and 55-65 in age. A 27
word list of one syllable was used, all of which rhymed with at least 2 other
English words but not with any other words in the test list. There were five
orienting procedures for the tasks, all self-paced, as follows: letter count, rhyme,
adjective, imagery, and control (intentional learning). Each task involved specific
instructions on what to do with the word list, and, immediately following list
removal, subjects were given 5 minutes to write their free recall responses.

Results indicate that recall for the younger subjects was significantly greater
than for the older group in tasks where more semantic processing was required.
The Age X Orienting Task interaction was significant ($p < .001$), which was
interpreted to mean that age related decrements are a function of increasing
semantic processing demands. In the orienting tasks that require semantic processing, such as the adjective and imagery tasks, the older group performed relatively poorly. In the nonsemantic tasks, recall scores were not significantly different.

An analysis of categorical clustering (clustering refers to the tendency of items
which are conceptually related to one another to be recalled together as a category) did not indicate significant age related differences in organization, which is
consistent with the findings of Hultsch (1971b), who demonstrated that the
elderly exhibit decrements in memory tasks which minimize the opportunity for
meaningful organization, but whose performance is observed to improve where
the opportunity is maximized.

It should be pointed out that, as is consistent with the findings of Hyde and
Jenkins (1973), both groups in the Eysenck study performed as well in incidental
learning as in intentional learning when the orienting tasks required semantic
processing.

Mode of Input

Several investigators have demonstrated that auditory presentation of material to be recalled is related to superior performance for adults when compared to

a visual source of input (Arenberg, 1968; McGhie, Chapman, & Lawson, 1965; Taub, 1972a).

Taub (1975) questioned the findings of these earlier studies on the basis that the input stimuli were limited to unrelated digits presented sequentially and that some of the studies used visual and auditory input modes in combination, thereby masking their independent effects. Taub (1975) therefore designed a study in which 66 subjects were divided equally into age groups of 19–31, 41–60, and 61–78 years. The stimuli consisted of six prose passages varying in length from 46 to 67 words. Material used for the digit span test were pairs of sequences at each of the lengths from 3 to 10 digits. Half of the subject in each group were presented (visually) both the digit and prose materials. The other half were presented task materials auditorially.

Results show that performance was better under the auditory condition for the digit span test, whereas the visual modality was related to better performance with the prose material. Modality effects were similar across age levels, although there were age related differences in both tasks and modes. Taub interpreted these findings to mean that additional research is needed to specify the nature of conditions of presentation and task demands before any general conclusions can be drawn regarding whether the auditory or visual mode is more beneficial to the aged.

Taub and Kline (1976) report three experiments designed to further evaluate modality effects in the aged when both prose passages and unrelated digits are used. Experiment I involved prose passages in the form of paragraphs ranging from 46 to 76 words in length which were either typed for visual presentation or taped for auditory presentation. Subsequent to presentation, each subject recalled verbally as much as possible. Subjects were divided into groups as follows: review and no review, experimenter- and subject-paced.

Experiments II and III utilized unrelated digit lists varying in length from three to eight (nine in Experiment III) digits which were either typed for presentation via a memory drum or taped for auditory presentation. Following a constant presentation rate of one digit per second, each subject was required to recall the digits in the exact order given. Subjects were divided into the following groups: sequential auditory presentation, sequential visual, sequential but with each successive digit placed in varying positions proceeding from left to right (thereby providing spatial cues paralleling reading conditions with no review), and simultaneous, in which all digits appeared together (analogous to reading condition with review possible).

The data indicate that modality choice related to specific presentation conditions rather than kind of stimulus materials. In Experiment II performance was better for the auditory mode as compared to the visual under sequential presentation with temporal cues. There were no differences in modalities when the visual presentation also had spatial cues as in Experiments I and II. Results from Experiments I and III indicate the visual mode was better than the auditory under read and review conditions. The authors suggest that the visual mode appears to be more appropriate for use in elderly training programs, since it provides an opportunity for review during reading (especially in real-life situations).

Primacy–Recency Effects. We discussed earlier the nature of the serial position effect as an invariant phenomenon. In free recall, words at the beginning (primacy) and words at the end (recency) are recalled more often than items in the middle of the list. Arenberg (1976) notes that different variables affect the primacy and recency portions of lists and that the auditory mode is related to better recall of items in the recency (STM) portion than is visual modality. He was therefore interested in the effects of auditory augmentation in free recall, with emphasis on the primacy portion (LTM).

There were 42 subjects in the young group, with an age range of 17 to 19 years, and 42 in the old group of range 60 to 70 years. Each subject was assigned to one of six possible orders of three presentation conditions. Four blocks of three lists were presented, the first consisting of three 8-word lists and the other three consisting of three 16-word lists. Presentation rate was 3 seconds per word. In the active auditory condition, the subject said the word aloud as it was presented. In the passive auditory condition, the experimenter said the word aloud while the subject listened. In the visual only condition, the subject simply looked at the stimulus. After presentation, subjects were instructed to write down the words they could recall at a self-paced rate.

Results were consistent with the earlier findings of Arenberg (1968) and McGhie *et al.* (1965) in that both groups benefited from the auditory presentation in recall of the recency portion; however, contrary to the earlier studies, the old did not realize more benefits than the young under the auditory mode.

The results for the primacy portion indicate that the ranking of means was the reverse for the ranking for recency. Active auditory was inferior to passive auditory, which was inferior to visual only. This held for both groups. These data are interpreted to mean that active vocalization of primacy items serves as interference to the processing required for their later recall.

For the elderly, the active auditory condition on recall of words in the primacy portion is additionally negative, since this condition requires the subject to alternate input and output operations, because reading and saying require alternating attention, which has been shown to be difficult for the aged. Arenberg submits that, since the active auditory augmentation is related to performance decrements in the elderly for the primacy portion when unrelated words are utilized, care should be taken to avoid this mode if similar decrement is found with related material used typically in an applied setting.

The findings of Taub (1975) are not consistent with Arenberg's (1976) data on passive auditory augmentation of primacy items. Taub reported that prose material was recalled better for all his groups when subjects silently read the material rather than having it read to them. Perhaps the fact that there was no review time in the Taub study contributed to performance decrements for all groups.

Arenberg (1977) reported a study on the effects of auditory cues on retention of nonverbal (geometric design) material in two groups of male subjects, one of mean age 18.0 and the other of mean age 65.5. He hypothesized that recall would improve as a function of auditory augmentation and that the old would benefit more from augmentation than would the young. In the visual condition, each of nine geometric designs were displayed for 12 seconds, and 15 seconds later the subject was asked to reproduce the design. In the auditory augmentation condition, the subject listened to a description of the design's salient features in addition to watching the display of the design. Two sets of designs were used. All subjects were presented with the first set under the visual condition. Then, for the second set, half the subjects in each group were tested in the visual condition and the other half in the auditory condition.

Results were interpreted as supportive of both hypotheses. Arenberg (1977) suggests that the description of the designs provided "both a rehearsable form of the design and additional retrieval cues. Rehearsal of nonverbal material . . . seems to depend upon a verbal encoding [p. 194]." Perhaps impairment in retrieval is a partial function of inadequate encoding of retrieval cues at input.

Visual Modality. A variation of the visual mode is to present stimulus materials in the form of pictures or printed words or both. Keitz and Gounard (1976) included this method in their design of a study in which 40 females were divided into two groups of mean ages 22.1 and 69.4. They learned 20-item lists of pictorial and printed word stimuli under untimed free recall conditions over eight trials. Results indicate that recall of pictures is superior, for both groups, to that of printed words, which supports the findings of Paivio (1971), and that the younger group made significantly fewer errors than the older group. Also, performance increments were realized by both groups as an increasing function of number of trials.

These data were interpreted to mean that memory functions for the visual and verbal modalities are related to quantitative, not qualitative differences with age. The authors concluded that these findings provide additional evidence that age differences in learning–memory performance are not a function of a basic change in underlying storage processes.

Registration

Arenberg (1965) designed a study in which two groups consisting of elderly and young subjects learned lists of paired associates either under a short or a long anticipation interval. The procedure also included sporadic times for self-paced trials, in which the stimulus word alone was presented with no response

time restrictions. Results indicated a reduction in errors under the longer anticipation interval. The decrease in errors under the self-paced condition was interpreted as being due to both the additional time to respond and the additional
time to prevent erasure, which related to Welford's (1959) hypothesis that the
STM mechanism of the elderly is affected negatively by incoming stimuli; that
is, that stimulus patterns are erased by incoming stimuli before some sort of consolidation process necessary for permanent storage is completed.

Canestrari (1968) performed a test of this erasure hypothesis by presenting
paired associate items to 152 subjects of age range 30–69 who were divided into
four groups of 10 year spans. The lists were of 10 one-syllable words and 10 response words. The intervals between presentations were .0 seconds, .5 seconds,
and 5.0 seconds. The pairs were exposed for 1 second. Each subject was given
the list and, upon completion of a run, they were presented with the stimulus
word for which there were no time restrictions to respond.

Results indicate significant age and interval differences ($p < .01$ and $p < .01$)
and Age $\times$ Interval interaction ($p < .05$). The author interpreted these interaction data as indicative of an age related deficit when the interval between pairs
is short, even under the unlimited response time. The age related decrement in
performance was due to an increase in errors of omission, which does not provide evidence supportive of an interference hypothesis. Canestrari suggested that
although these data did not confirm the erasure hypothesis, they are not contradictory to it. It should be pointed out that the performance of the 60–69 age
group reflected the most gains as a function of increased interitem intervals.

Hulicka and Wheeler (1976) suggest that the old would benefit more than the
young from the addition of a registration interval and therefore hypothesized
that older adults required more time than younger persons to register information or to transfer it from STM to LTM. To test this hypothesis, 24 persons of
mean age 69.17 and 24 persons of mean age 19.34 participated in a paired
associate study in which they were asked to recall four lists of either 10 or 20
pairs of nouns under the following conditions: (a) 3-second study interval, no
registration; (b) self-paced study, no registration interval; (c) self-paced study
interval, 4-second registration interval; and (d) self-paced study and registration
intervals. The anticipation interval was self-paced under all conditions.

Results were interpreted as supportive of the hypothesis, presumably because
the registration interval provided the time necessary for information to be transferred into LTM or reduced the extent of erasure of material while it was still in
STM, or both.

The data of this study were interpreted as further evidence for age related
deficits in paired associate tasks as a function of learning, not performance, factors. The findings were also considered as consistent with Birren's (1974) notion
that old persons most likely *need* more time to process information because of a
basic change (i.e., a slowing down) in the speed with which the central nervous

system processes material. Finally, the authors point out that significant improvement in the older adult's performance can be realized through modification of learning performance conditions.

Mediators and Organization

Canestrari (1968) also conducted a study to determine the effects of verbal and visual mediators on acquisition. It had been shown earlier that the elderly do not use mediators (which could interfere with secondary storage encoding processes) to the extent of younger subjects and that when mediators are introduced into paired associate conditions, performance increments for the elderly were observed (Hulicka & Grossman, 1967). Investigators also suggested that the improvement in performance of the elderly under increased stimulus intervals could be due to the fact that they have additional time to form mediators.

Briefly, learners encode or otherwise process information presented to them according to individual strategies, of which an important aspect is the nature of the organization of the input. Earlier we discussed the central process hypothesis of Atkinson and Shiffrin (1968), which posits two features of processing, namely, fixed structural features and control processes. Arenberg and Robertson (1974) pointed out that age differences in learning performance are to some extent a function of differences in the utilization of control processes. These control processes involve both the organization of information according to specific groupings and classifications and the use of mediators, such as mnemonics, to the organization. Robertson-Tchabo, Hausman, and Arenberg (1976) conducted studies in which older adults were trained and encouraged to use a mnemonic device effectively in free recall tasks.

In the mediator experiment of Canestrari (1968), 30 subjects of age range 50–73 and 30 of age range 16–27 were presented with 30 one-syllable stimulus words paired with 30 response words, which were divided into three lists. Sketches (visual mediators) were drawn that depicted the word pairs. Short phrases (verbal mediators) described each word pair.

Results indicate that the younger group made significantly fewer errors than the older group. There was a significant Age X Treatment interaction. The reduction in errors through the use of both mediators was greater in the older group. Analysis of commission and omission errors indicates that the usage of the mediators had no significant effect on reduction of commission errors but had a significant effect on omission errors. These data could be interpreted to mean that the mediators provide the association link required for efficient storage processes and that in addition the mediators raised their confidence to respond, since they were more certain that they would emit the correct response.

In the two studies of Robertson-Tchabo, Hausman, and Arenberg (1976), subjects ranging in age from 38 to 84 were trained to use the method of loci in free recall of word lists. This mnemonic device involves the association of words to be recalled with specific locations (loci) provided by subjects as part of their daily environment. They were simply to visualize (in the mind's eye, so to speak) a word as in association with a highly familiar place. The authors point out that these loci are strong retrieval cues of a nonredundant nature. In addition, this particular method of loci tends to reduce interference both at the input phase and at recall.

In both studies performance increments were realized by subjects who readily learned this method, which presumably facilitates recall both by improving the encoding process through organization and by utilizing loci to provide retrieval cues functional at the search phase of recall.

Treat and Reese (1976) report a study in which two groups of subjects (mean ages of 29.7 and 69.6) learned meaningful noun pairs under varying anticipation and presentation intervals. Subjects were divided into experimenter-provided imagery, self-generated imagery, and combined groups. Results indicate that both age groups benefited when instructions for using imagery in connecting the word pairs presented via a memory drum were given. When the imagery was self-generated under long anticipation interval conditions, the older group performed as well as the younger. Both groups' performance reflected decrement under no imagery instructions and short anticipation intervals. Under combined conditions the performance of the young was superior to that of the old. The data were interpreted to mean that the young required the longer anticipation time only in the absence of imagery; however, the old needed it in order to profit from imagery instructions. These authors suggest the old have ability comparable to that of the young to generate and use imagery, although the old need longer time for retrieval.

Some investigators have provided evidence contrary to the hypothesized age related deficits in registration (Inglis, Sykes, & Ankus, 1968; Monge & Hultsch, 1971; Taub, 1968; Taub & Grieff, 1967). Data indicated age related performance deficits for only the second half span of the material to be remembered. Taub (1968) designed two experiments to determine the nature of the effects of several variables on the first and second half performance of young and elderly people. Each stimulus sequence included six or eight black letters; half of each were coded with either a red or a green background. The coding was to have the effect of providing some sort of anchor for which half span to recall first. There were two presentation rates for each letter, 1 second and 2 seconds, with an interstimulus time of .05 seconds.

The most significant findings were that age related differences were observed only in the second half reports and that there were no other age interactions with the other variables. The author suggests that age related decrements lie not in the "ability to reorganize and rehearse one or more sets of material in memory but in the ability to maintain that organization once a response has been initiated [p. 163]." The author interprets these data as consistent with an interference model and as evidence for the idea that age related deficits are a function of response interference.

It would appear that both half spans are stored. If so, then the first half is stored for a relatively short time and is therefore not susceptible to interference from response effects. On the other hand, the second half span is stored for a longer period of time and is both susceptible to decay and to interference when the first half is recalled. It is understood that total registration of half spans is essential when recall begins.

Taub (1972b) replicated his earlier studies in order to determine if these initial findings were related to a methodological error in equating groups. The present findings support the 1967 and 1968 data.

Retrieval

Schonfield (1965, 1967) suggested that age related deficits in recall are due to problems in retrieval from storage rather than to a storage deficit. To illustrate this, Schonfield and Robertson (1966) presented to 134 subjects of age range 20–75 two lists, each of 24 nouns or adjectives for recall or recognition. The authors hypothesized that recognition scores would not reflect decrement to the degree of recall. Subjects were instructed either to recall as many words in any order as possible (free recall) or instructed to underline one word in any group of five that were initially presented (recognition test). Subjects were tested for recognition on one list and for recall on the other list.

Results show no decrement on the recognition scores but a marked decrease in recall scores. These data were interpreted to mean that there are age related deficits in retrieval from storage (as supported by age differences in recall scores, which are a function of search and retrieval processes, while recognition, for which there are no differences, does not involve retrieval).

The authors suggested two strategies that would tend to neutralize the effects of a retrieval deficit. First, the elderly should plan ahead for events so as to focus attention through rehearsal, and, second, the number of stimulus cues related to whatever is stored should be increased.

Laurence (1967) designed an experiment to test these strategies suggested by Schonfield. Thirty subjects of mean age 75 served in Experiment I and 28 in Experiment II. The first experiment tested Schonfield's rehearsal strategy, in which it was hypothesized that if subjects were given category names for the words in the test lists they could rehearse them prior to the test and get the benefits of this organizational procedure, which would be reflected in facilitated recall. Results did not support the hypothesis. It was suggested that this was due to the 2-second presentation rate, wherein rehearsal time was virtually eliminated.

The second experiment involved cue at recall, in which subjects were given cue cards prior to the recall test. Results indicate no significant differences between the two groups' scores, which is contrary to the typical finding of age differences in performance. The authors interpreted these findings as favorable to the Schonfield hypothesis that the memory deficit is related to an impairment in retrieval. This is consistent with Tulving and Pearlstone (1966), who submit that some stored information is available but not accessible and that differences in availability and accessibility are a partial function of a deficit in retrieval operations and not of impaired storage.

McNulty and Caird (1966), however, explain the elderly's difficulty in recall as a function of getting material into storage initially. They questioned the Schofield interpretations and suggested that despite the data demonstrating stabilized recognition scores, an absence of differences in the amount of material stored by the age groups has not been demonstrated. McNulty and Caird suggest that in a recognition task, all that is necessary to identify the correct response is partial information. In other words, just a portion of the input must be stored in order to identify (recognize) the total input under later test conditions. These authors suggested that recognition scores are inflated because of partial learning.

Hartley and Marshall (1967) followed through on McNulty and Caird's suggestion and designed a study in which a series of recognition tests would increasingly require complete learning of the items in the lists, under the assumption that the results of recognition tests in which correct and incorrect choices are designed to be more and more similar should be differentially influenced by age.

Two lists of 12 words which contained distractors were presented to 13 elderly subjects of age range 70–85. Results indicate no significant differences in recognition scores between the two lists, which places the McNulty–Caird objections in doubt, although the authors did suggest that there may be another, more efficient way to tease out partial learning. The question of what parts of the material to be remembered are being stored remains unresolved.

In order to provide direct evidence bearing on the storage versus retrieval controversy, Drachman and Leavitt (1972) conducted a series of experiments on groups of elderly and young subjects. The experimental group was composed of 24 subjects with a mean age of 66.8 years, whereas the control group consisted of 24 subjects with a mean age of 21.8.

The subjects were tested individually in one experimental session of about 2 hours. A single trial digit span starting with four digits was presented, and subjects proceeded until they could no longer recall a sequence perfectly. The longest sequence of perfect repetition was their digit span. The supraspan digit test consisted of repeated presentation of each of five sequences of 15 digits. The cued and uncued multitrial free recall test consisted of two lists of 35 words each, with the initial letters of the words serving as cues. Subjects were tested under both conditions, and recall was self-paced and written. The retrieval by category test consisted of the name of a familiar category of nouns, such as "flowers." Subjects were to say as many words to fit the categories as they could, and as quickly as possible.

Results indicate that first letter cuing of word lists at recall did benefit all subjects but did not provide a significantly greater advantage for the elderly. It was suggested earlier that cuing should be related to a greater recall advantage for the elderly, who have a retrieval impairment. These present data suggest that retrieval in the aged was comparatively unimpaired.

Of particular interest, however, is the fact that the retrieval by category data showed no significant deficit in the older group. The authors point out that this is the only direct test of retrieval in the series and that "intactness of performance is a strong indication that retrieval, at least from old memory stores, is unimpaired [p. 306]."

The immediate memory span data indicate no significant deficit; however, the supraspan data indicate a significant decrement. The authors interpret these data as supportive of storage impairment, rather than a retrieval deficit, as a significant factor in the aged's memory difficulties.

Search and Retrieval

Anders, Fozard, and Lillyquist (1972) provide evidence on the nature of retrieval operations in STM. The search process in retrieval has been characterized as exhaustive (subjects scan the entire list on virtually all occasions), serial (proceeds through item by item), and very fast (about 25 items per second). The present study involved thirty subjects divided equally into three age ranges of 19–21, 33–43, and 58–85. On each trial the subject was presented with lists of one, three, five, or seven digits to be remembered. The lists were presented visually at a rate of one per second. The task was to decide whether or not the digit appeared in an earlier presentation and to indicate the answer by depressing as rapidly as possible a yes or no switch.

Results indicate that the yes and no response latencies were similar for the groups, which is interpreted to mean that the entire list undergoes search for both conditions. It appeared also that all subjects conducted a serial and exhaustive search of material in STM. The authors suggest that an exhaustive search indicates that retrieval time is a function of list length. Search speed was observed as decreasing function of age; that is, the younger subjects were significantly faster in search speed.

The authors point out that short lists of digits were utilized to insure that all subjects could register and store the lists with equal facility, thereby yielding an independent measure of retrieval operations. The low error score data indicate that all items were registered and stored. These data were interpreted to mean that, as the items in store increase, more time in search is required. As indicated, the elderly's search speed is significantly slower, which of course is related to a retrieval deficit.

SUMMARY AND CONCLUSIONS

There have been a number of questions, both experimental and theoretical, raised throughout this and the preceding chapters to which no definitive answers have been given. This is understandable since, for one reason, a coherent, unified position on the nature of memory is nonexistent, in spite of nearly 100 years of research. In addition, investigators have been dealing with the brain, the most complicated system known, thereby partially accounting for the present situation of ambiguity and incompleteness. On the other hand, perhaps unifying, general principles are not to be found despite similarities in underlying mechanisms, and we shall simply have to be satisfied with manipulating experimental and environmental variables in our efforts to identify processes and antecedents of memory functions.

For example, the many studies on the nature of interference conducted since the time of Ebbinghaus have failed to explain to everyone's satisfaction the enormously complex processes that produce interference effects. Also unanswered is the question whether forgetting is a function of decay with time or of new memories having been superimposed on the old.

Although different storage systems have been operationally defined, profound doubts remain as to whether there is indeed more than one memory store with definitive characteristics. Presumably, STM has a limited capacity of between four and eight items which are subject to rapid decay without rehearsal, whereas LTM has unlimited storage potential of a relatively permanent nature.

Some investigators suggest that the *sound* of a word is what is stored in STM, wheras only *meaning* is stored in LTM. From another perspective, memory is not construed as having two functionally distinct stores, but rather it is thought that what is contained in memory is related to its level of processing, that is, to how deeply the material to be stored is processed, so that storage is an increasing function of the quantitative and qualitative aspects of processing itself. As degree of processing increases, so do the number of connections with current storage, which in turn increases the probability that that which is being processed will be retained in memory.

Another problematic area related to the limitations of learning and memory research concerns the fact that an individual will utilize a variety of personal as well as experimentally induced strategies at any given time in learning–memory tasks, and the nature of these strategies is highly inferential, since the experimenter's control is virtually limited to observable input and output (despite experimental instructions).

In any case, a consistent finding reported in the literature of learning and memory in the aged is that the elderly's performance reflects impairment under either input, storage, or output conditions when they are required to alternate (divide) attention or reorganize task materials.

Memory span studies, which typically test PM, show negligible differences in performance with age; however, even in these studies, if the older person is required to alternate attention or to reorganize material, then performance decrement is observed.

Performance increments are observed under auditory modality conditions; however, the older person does not appear to benefit more (i.e., significantly more) than the younger person under auditory mode of presentation conditions; the exception, however, is found when the elderly must divide attention. Under these conditions, they benefit more than their younger counterparts.

Performance is observed to be an increasing function of the number and quality of retrieval cues present at recall in SM (LTM) tasks. As retrieval cues increase (which reduces the amount of information to be generated), performance increments are observed.

Older persons tend to benefit more from instructions to form and use mediators in the organization of information to be recalled. Some investigators report that despite experimental instructions many elderly subjects do not actually follow through on them, presumably because they are not capable of deep processing. Thus, performance decrements in SM are viewed to be a partial function of impairment in acquisition; that is, information is not efficiently processed through mental operations, which leads to retention decrements.

The evidence seems to support (albeit tentatively) the notion that the elderly are more susceptible to interference effects, so that trace strength is attenuated by prior or subsequent learning.

Based on the experimental studies of learning and memory discussed, I should like to make the following additional, specific recommendations to educational gerontologists who are working in applied settings or are designing learning environments:

1. Interference from response competition should be reduced through minimization of response alternatives or complexity of cues at recall.
2. Material to be recalled (learned) should be retained at maximum strength before new material is introduced.
3. Auditory and visual augmentation procedures should be fully utilized for better retention.
4. Instructions to use and aid to form mediators should augment any program of learning for the elderly, since mediators tend to neutralize the organizational deficits observed in their performance.
5. Whatever is to be remembered should be made meaningful, in contrast to nonsensical, since the older learner appears to perform better in these kinds of situations.
6. Finally, and perhaps most important, the speed with which a task is carried out should be reduced to meet the sensory slowing down in the aged.

AN ALTERNATE FRAMEWORK

Thus far we have focused our discussions on the S-R (associative) and information processing (and variants thereof) approaches to the study of learning and
memory. In the former, learning is defined by stimulus–response associations
which become the content of memory. Learning and memory are viewed as following a relentless path of irreversible decline, in which interference and decay
are inextricably related to biological mechanisms. In the latter, learning and
memory are construed to be a function of storage mechanisms and control processes, in which decline is predictable but modifiable through experimental manipulation.

Jenkins (1974) has suggested a contextualist approach to memory as being
more nearly valid than the other approaches dominant (mainly the traditional
associative one) heretofore. This view submits that what memory is depends on
context. According to Jenkins, learning and memory are functions of (a) the
physical and psychological context in which the event to be remembered was
experienced; (b) the abilities one expresses in the recall context; (c) recall conditions; and (d) the relationship of task–experimenter demands to what one
remembers, so that what is learned and remembered in any situation is related to
its total context. Emphasis is simply placed on the event (which involves ecologi-
cally valid practical problems), not the *machine.*

The contextual approach suggests that decrement in learning and memory is
not necessarily concomitant with aging. Although published research emanating
from within this perspective is virtually nonexistent, Jenkins submits that memory research is progressing toward contextualism. Hultsch (1977) points out that
the approach would appear useful (not as the single thrust, but as part of a plu-
ralistic mode) in the study of adult performance, since traditional physical science models, with their insistence on general laws and lack of emphasis on interaction effects, seem inappropriate in the analysis of human behavior.

REFERENCES

AGRUSO, V. M. JR., & RECKASE, M. D. The relative difficulty position function. *British
    Journal of Psychology,* 1976, *67,* 569-577.
ANDERS T. R., FOZARD, J. L., & LILLYQUIST, T. D. Effects of age upon retrieval from
    short term memory. *Developmental Psychology,* 1972, *6,* 214-217.
ARENBERG, D. Anticipation interval and age differences in verbal learning. *Journal of
    Abnormal Psychology,* 1965, *70,* 419-425.
ARENBERG, D. Input modality in short term retention of old and young adults. *Journal
    of Gerontology,* 1968, *23,* 462-465.
ARENBERG, D. The effects of input condition on free recall in young and old adults. *Jour-
    nal of Gerontology,* 1976, *31,* 551-555.

ARENBERG, D. The effects of auditory augmentation on visual retention for young and old adults. *Journal of Gerontology*, 1977, *32*, 192-195.

ARENBERG, D., & ROBERTSON, E. A. The older individual as a learner. In S. M. Grubowski & W. D. Mason (Eds.), *Education for the aging*. Washington, D.C.: Capital Publications, 1974.

ATKINSON, R. C., & SHIFFRIN, R. M. Human memory: A proposed system and its control processes. In K. W. Spence & J. T. Spence (Eds.), *The psychology of learning and motivation*, Vol. 2. New York: Academic Press, 1968.

BIRREN, J. E. Translations from gerontology—From lab to life. Psychophysiology and speed of response. *American Psychologist*, 1974, *29*, 808-815.

BOTWINICK, J. *Cognitive processes in maturity and old age*. New York: Springer, 1967.

BROWN, J. Some tests of the decay theory of immediate memory. *Quarterly Journal of Experimental Psychology*, 1958, *10*, 12-21.

CANESTRARI, R. E. JR. Age changes in acquisition. In G. A. Talland (Ed.), *Human aging and behavior: Recent advances in research and theory*. New York: Academic Press, 1968.

CRAIK, F. I. M. Short term memory and the aging process. In G. A. Talland (Ed.), *Human aging and behavior: Recent advances in research and theory*. New York: Academic Press, 1968.

CRAIK, F. I. M., & LOCKHART, R. S. Levels of processing: A framework for memory research. *Journal of Verbal Learning and Verbal Behavior*, 1972, *11*, 671-684.

CRAIK, F. I. M., & MASANI, P. A. Age differences in temporal integration of language. *British Journal of Psychology*, 1967, *58*, 291-299.

CRAIK, F. I. M., & MASANI, P. A. Age and intelligence differences in coding and retrieval of word lists. *British Journal of Psychology*, 1969, *60*, 315-319.

CRAIK, F. I. M., & TULVING, E. Depth of processing and the retention of words in episodic memory. *Journal of Experimental Psychology: General*, 1975, *104*, 268-294.

DEUTSCH, J. A. The physiological basis of memory. *Annual Review of Psychology*, 1969, *20*, 85-104.

DRACHMAN, D. A., & LEAVITT, J. Memory impairment in the aged. Storage versus retrieval deficit. *Journal of Experimental Psychology*, 1972, *93*, 302-308.

EBBINGHAUS, H. *Memory: A contribution to experimental psychology*. Translated by H. A. Ruger & C. E. Bussemius. New York: Dover, 1964.

ENESCO, H. E. RNA and memory: A re-evaluation of the present data. *Canadian Psychiatric Association Journal*, 1967, *12*, 29-34.

EYSENCK, M. W. Age differences in incidental learning. *Developmental Psychology*, 1974, *10*, 936-941.

GILBERT, J. G. Memory loss in senescence. *Journal of Abnormal and Social Psychology*, 1941, *36*, 73-86.

GLADIS, M., & BRAUN, H. W. Age differences in transfer and retroaction as a function of intertask response similarity. *Journal of Experimental Psychology*, 1958, *55*, 25-30.

GLANZER, M., & CUNITZ, A. R. Two storage mechanisms in free recall. *Journal of Verbal Learning and Verbal Behavior*, 1966, *5*, 351-360.

HARTLEY, J., & MARSHALL, I. S. Aging, recognition and partial learning. *Psychonomic Science*, 1967, *9*(4).

HAVINGHURST, R. J., & GLASSER, R. An exploratory study of reminiscence. *Journal of Gerontology*, 1972, *27*, 245-253.

HEBB, D. O. *The organization of behavior.* New York: Wiley, 1949.

HEBB, D. O. Distinctive features of learning in the higher animal. In J. F. Delafresnaye (Ed.), *Brain mechanisms and learning.* Oxford, England: Blackwell Scientific, 1961.

HEBB, D. O. *Textbook of psychology.* Philadelphia: Saunders, 1972.

HILGARD, E. Introduction to Dover Edition of Hermann Ebbinghaus' *Memory: A contribution to experimental psychology.* Translated by Henry A. Ruger and Clara E. Bussenius. New York: Dover, 1964.

HULICKA, I. M. Age differences in Wechsler Memory Scale scores. *Journal of Genetic Psychology,* 1966, 135–145.

HULICKA, I. M., & GROSSMAN, J. L. Age group comparisons for the use of mediators in paired associate learning. *Journal of Gerontology,* 1967, *22,* 46–51.

HULICKA, I. M., & WEISS, R. L. Age differences in retention as a function of learning. *Journal of Consulting Psychology,* 1965, *29,* 125–129.

HULICKA, I. M., & WHEELER, D. Recall scores of old and young people as a function of registration intervals. *Educational Gerontology,* 1976, *1,* 361–372.

HULTSCH, D. Adult age differences in free classification and free recall. *Developmental Psychology,* 1971, *4,* 338–342. (b)

HULTSCH, D. Organization and memory in adulthood. *Human Development,* 1971, *14,* 16–29. (a)

HULTSCH, D. F. Changing perspectives on basic research in adult learning and memory. *Educational Gerontology: An International Quarterly,* 1977, *2,* 367–382.

HYDE, T. S., & JENKINS, J. J. Recall for words as a function of semantic, graphic, and syntactic orienting tasks. *Journal of Verbal Learning and Verbal Behavior,* 1973, *12,* 471–480.

INGLIS, J., SYKES, D. H., & ANKUS, M. N. Age differences in short term memory. In S. Chown & K. F. Riegel (Eds.), *Interdisciplinary Topics in Gerontology,* Vol. 1. New York: Karger, 1968.

JENKINS, J. J. Remember that old theory of memory? Well, forget it. *American Psychologist,* 1974, *29,* 785–795.

JEROME, E. A. Age and learning—Experimental studies. In J. E. Birren (Ed.), *Handbook of aging and the individual.* Chicago: University of Chicago Press, 1959. Pp. 655–699.

KEITZ, S. M., & GOUNARD, B. R. Age differences in adults' free recall of pictorial and word stimuli. *Educational Gerontology: An International Quarterly,* 1976, *1,* 237–241.

KRIAUCIUNAS, R. Short term memory and age. *Journal of the American Geriatrics Society,* 1968, *16,* 83–93.

LASHLEY, K. S. In search of the engram. In F. A. Beach, D. O. Hebb, C. T. Morgan, & H. W. Nissen (Eds.), *The neuropsychology of Lashley.* New York: McGraw-Hill, 1960.

LAURENCE, M. W. Memory loss with age: A test of two strategies for its retardation. *Psychonomic Science,* 1967, *9,* 209–210.

MANDLER, G. Organization and memory. In K. W. Spence & J. T. Spence (Eds.), *The Psychology of learning and motiviation: Advances in research and theory.* New York: Academic Press, 1, 1967. (a)

MANDLER, G. Verbal learning. In *New directions in psychology.* New York: Holt, 1967. (b)

MCGEOGH, J. A., & IRION, A. L. *The psychology of human learning.* New York: McKay, 1952.

MCGHIE, A. N., CHAPMAN, J., & LAWSON, J. S. Changes in immediate memory with age. *British Journal of Psychology,* 1965, *56,* 69-75.

MCNULTY, J. A., & CAIRD, W. Memory loss with age: Retrieval or storage? *Psychological Reports,* 1966, *19,* 229-230.

MELTON, A. W. Implications of short term memory for a general theory of memory. *Journal of Verbal Learning and Verbal Behavior,* 1963, *2,* 1-21.

MOENSTER, P. A. Learning and memory in relation to age. *Journal of Gerontology,* 1972, *27,* 361-363.

MONGE, R., & HULTSCH, D. Paired associate learning as a function of adult age and the length of the anticipation and inspection intervals. *Journal of Gerontology,* 1971, *26,* 157-162.

MURDOCK, B. B. JR. The distinctiveness of stimuli. *Psychological Review,* 1960, *67,* 16-31.

PAIVIO, A. *Imagery and verbal processes.* New York: Holt, Rinehart and Winston, 1971.

PENFIELD, W. The permanent record of the stream of consciousness. In *Proceedings of the 14th International Congress of Psychology,* 1954, Pp. 47-69.

PENFIELD, W. Consciousness, memory, and man's conditioned reflexes. In Karl H. Pribram (Ed.), *On the biology of learning.* New York: Harcourt, 1969.

PETERSON, L. R., & PETERSON, M. J. Short term retention of individual verbal items. *Journal of Experimental Psychology,* 1959, *58,* 193-198.

PRIBRAM, K. H. The four r's of remembering. In K. H. Pribram (Ed.), *On the biology of of learning.* New York: Harcourt, 1969.

PRIBRAM, K. H. The neurophysiology of remembering. In *Readings from Scientific American: Physiological psychology.* San Francisco: W. H. Freeman, 1972.

PRIBRAM, K. H., NUWER, M., & BARON, R. J. The holographic hypothesis of memory structure in brain function and perception. In D. H. Krantz, R. C. Atkinson, R. D. Luce, & P. Suppes (Eds.), *Contemporary developments in mathematical psychology,* Vol. II. San Francisco: W. H. Freeman, 1974.

ROBERTSON-TCHABO, E. A. R., HAUSMAN, C. P., & ARENBERG, D. A classic mnemonic for older learners: A trip that works! *Educational Gerontology,* 1976, *1,* 215-226.

ROSENZWEIG, M. R., BENNETT, E. L., & DIAMOND, M. C. Brain changes in response to experience, *Scientific American,* 1972, *226*(2), 22-29.

SCHONFIELD, D. Memory changes with age. *Nature,* 1965, *28,* 918.

SCHONFIELD, D. Memory loss with age: Acquisition and retrieval. *Psychological Reports,* 1967, *20,* 223-226.

SCHONFIELD, D., & ROBERTSON, E. A. Memory storage and aging. *Canadian Journal of Psychology,* 1966, *20,* 228-236.

SPERLING, G. The information available in brief visual presentations. *Psychological Monographs,* 1960, *74,* No. 498 .

TALLAND, G. A. Three estimates of word span and their stability over the adult years. *Quarterly Journal of Experimental Psychology,* 1965, *17,* 301-307.

TALLAND, G. A. Age and the span of immediate recall. In G. A. Talland (Ed.), *Human aging and behavior: Recent advances in research and theory.* New York: Academic Press, 1968.

TAUB, H. A. Age differences in memory as a function of rate of presentation, order of report, and stimulus organization. *Journal of Gerontology*, 1968, *23*, 159-164.

TAUB, H. A. A comparison of young adult and old groups on various digit span tasks. *Developmental Psychology*, 1972, *6*, 60-65. (a)

TAUB, H. A. A further study of aging, short term memory and complexity of stimulus organization. *Journal of Genetic Psychology*, 1972, *120*, 163-164.(b)

TAUB, H. A. Mode of presentation, age and short term memory. *Journal of Gerontology*, 1975, *30*(1), 56-59.

TAUB, H. A., & KLINE, G. E. Modality effects and memory in the aged. *Educational Gerontology: An International Quarterly*, 1976, *1*, 53-60.

TAUB, H. A., & GRIEFF, S. Effects of age on organization and recall of two sets of stimuli. *Psychonomic Science*, 1967, *7*, 53-54.

TREAT, N. J., & REESE, H. W. Age, pacing and imagery in paired-associate learning. *Developmental Psychology*, 1976, *12*, 119-124.

TULVING, E., & PEARLSTONE, Z. Availability versus accessibility of information in memory for words. *Journal of Verbal Learning and Verbal Behavior*, 1966,*5*, 381-391.

WAUGH, N. C., & NORMAN, D. A. Primary memory. *Psychological Review*, 1965, *72*, 89-104.

WECHSLER, D. *The measurement of adult intelligence*, 3rd ed. Baltimore: Williams and Wilkins Co., 1944.

WELFORD, A. T. Psychomotor performance. In J. E. Birren (Ed.), *Handbook of aging and the individual*. Chicago: University of Chicago Press, 1959, Pp. 562-613.

WIMER, R. E., & WIGDOR, B. T. Age differences in retention of learning. *Journal of Gerontology*, 1958, *13*, 291-295.

4

Intelligence

The final construct in our discussion is that of intelligence, for which no universally accepted definition is to be found. And although intelligence and its presumed overt index, the intelligence quotient (IQ), are overworked terms in our everyday vocabulary, we have yet to define them to everyone's satisfaction despite the fact that everyone "knows" what constitutes intelligent behavior.

Apparently, there are wide individual differences in the extent to which one describes behavior as intelligent. We have been wont to describe and explain certain aspects of that behavior by the term intelligence; however, it would appear fallacious to suggest that intelligence caused the behavior. The many definitions of intelligence describe certain aspects of the behavior under observation so that, put simply, one is left with the problem of deciding, for example, whether intelligent behavior is defined by the ability to abstract or by the ability to profit from experience or to otherwise learn? Traditional measures of intelligence operationally define intelligence as whatever a specific test measures. It is beyond the purview of this text to discuss the enormously complicated theoretical issues surrounding the degree to which it is related to neurobiological influences.

Obviously, one's behavior is influenced by operations of the central nervous system, which is a function of heredity and maturational (disease) factors.

Rather, my concern is with the nature and, more specifically, with the variability (as contrasted with the stability) in the elderly's ability to learn whatever is necessary for their adaptation to the environmental contingencies characterizing their present condition. In short, my interest is in environmental influences and in the modifiability of experimentally derived (and natural) learning or performance deficits, so that whatever the unmeasurable capacity or potential, its probability of being realized will have been increased.

It is not the intent of this chapter to attempt to articulate a link between the experimental and correlational approaches, either in the investigation of age related variables or in the interpretation of data generated from the learning, cognitive, and maturational models. This problem would appear better left to the developmental and experimental psychology of aging. Instead, I shall focus on the experimental studies dealing with problem solving and those factors capable of modification through various manipulative or intervention procedures. It is essential, of course, that the reader become familiar with the longitudinal, cross-sectional, and cross-sequential studies which have investigated the stability of intelligence, for which I shall now present an overview.

AGING AND INTELLIGENCE

One issue that pervades the literature of gerontology deals with the question of whether or not intelligence declines in old age. Volumes have been written in which studies have provided evidence supportive of, not supportive of, or as contradictory to belief in a decline in intelligence with age; however, a critical analysis of the empirical data leads this author to believe that some decline in some cognitive functions is an invariant phenomenon of the aging process (the reversibility of these changes is discussed in later sections). Contingent upon the definition of intelligence and the research paradigm utilized by the investigator, specific intellectual functions at specific age intervals have been (qualifiably) observed to change or otherwise to stabilize. A specific cognitive function observed to change is related to the kind of test given to the examinee. If performance, for example, on a vocabulary or information test is measured, then the performance score will hold well into the later years. On the other hand, the same individual's performance might be observed to decline or to not hold at a much earlier period if a perceptual-motor test is given. The problem lies in one's definition of intelligence.

Intelligence is viewed as capacity, a theoretical limit to one's performance, genetically determined (Botwinick, 1977), which is never actually measured, since performance is always somewhat lower than the capacity limits (Birren,

1959). If is also defined as ability, in which definition the focus is on one's present learning performance and relative ability, without reference to genetic endowment.

Performance scores are also influenced by such factors as proneness to fatigability over a long testing period (Furry & Baltes, 1973); however, as Botwinick (1977) points out, if performance is viewed in ability terms, then fatigue is not ability extraneous. Educational background is also a significant factor accounting for some of the variance in test performance (Granick & Friedman, 1973), along with socioeconomic status and cohort variables. Botwinick (1977) suggests that these latter factors may be of more significance than age itself. Or perhaps virtually all age changes in intelligence (of the sort we measure) are related to the cumulative effects of insult to the nervous system emanating from an inordinate number of potentially damaging stimuli, such as those produced by a highly industrialized, technologically oriented culture to which the human organism is exposed.

Cross-Sectional Studies[1]

Wechsler (1958) constructed tests of adult intelligence (Wechsler Bellevue and Wechsler Adult Intelligence Scale [WAIS]) that became the instrument of choice for most investigators studying the problems of decline in intelligence with age. The WAIS consists of eleven subtests which measure verbal ability and performance ability. Some of the tests require mainly problem solving or reasoning skills, whereas others rely heavily on one's information store and experiential background.

Wechsler found that results from the tests of verbal ability did not indicate significant differences among age groups; however, those tests which demanded reasoning ability yielded significant age differences. He called the verbal portion (vocabulary, information, object assembly, picture completion) "hold tests" and the performance portion (digit span, similarities, digit symbol, block design) "don't hold tests," to indicate that the former do not drop at the rate of the latter; that is, the performance indices of the performance tests show a significant decline with age. That the elderly score higher on the verbal than on the performance portion of the test has become known as the "classic aging pattern," since this finding has been found many times under a wide variety of conditions. Wechsler points out, however, that correlations (.40-.50) between age and intelligence are low, and, therefore, age itself accounts for only about 20-25% of the variance.

A major theory of intelligence followed shortly after the Wechsler work; it defined two fundamental types of intelligence, *fluid* and *crystallized* (Cattell,

[1]Botwinick (1967, 1977) provides exhaustive reviews.

1963). Fluid intelligence refers to a biological or genetic component and is therefore relatively independent of the effects of education, while crystallized intelligence refers to that which has been learned or otherwise accumulated through
experience. The former develops up into the late teens, whereas the latter develops over the years and shows little or no decline and even in some cases an increase.

Fluid intelligence is the capacity for acquiring new ideas, for grasping relationships, and for adapting to novel conditions; in other words, it is "brightness."
Crystallized intelligence is the investment of fluid intelligence in higher order
intellectual skills which one has had access to through environmental conditions,
that is, through the education provided by a particular culture. (Cattell suggests
that abilities related to fluid intelligence are functional from a network of cortical association areas, and that performance decrement in this type of intelligence
is proportional to the extent of injury or deterioration of these cortical areas. Of
course, this notion receives support from Lashley's Law of Mass Action, discussed in Chapter 3.)

Horn and Cattell (1967) constructed tests similar to those of Wechsler and
found that test scores measuring fluid skills corresponded to performance scores
on the Wechsler tests, both showing a decline with age. The crystallized intelligence tests yield scores comparable to the verbal scores of Wechsler.

In sum, Cattell (1971) provides evidence that the two types of intelligence are
reflected differently in growth curves over the years. Through the teenage years,
both types yield virtually identical curves; however, from this point on fluid
measures show a steady decline, whereas crystallized measures more or less indicate stabilization. Some investigators would interpret this rapid decline in fluid
ability as being related to the older adults' difficulty in acquiring new concepts
or in otherwise adapting to situations not previously experienced. The theory
does not advance invariant decline in fluid ability for every individual, since cortical deterioration varies with the health state of an individual despite the fact
that as one ages there is more susceptibility to disease or injury affecting the
brain structures involved in cognition. In other words, the theory is couched in
probability statements, which of course take into account individual differences.
Their findings have been interpreted (on the basis of data derived from cross-
sectional studies) as consistent with the classic aging pattern.

Botwinick (1977) points out that these studies show a performance decline in
psychomotor tests, especially under speeded conditions, whereas verbal functions remain relatively stable. Specifically, the verbal subtests of the WAIS, those
on information and vocabulary, show the least age differences of all the subtests.
The picture arrangement and digit symbol sections among the performance subtests show the greatest decrement of all subtests. Some investigators have interpreted these findings as indicating no decline, since these tests involve speed for
their successful completion. In general, the WAIS subtests show the beginning

of a significant decline between the ages of 45 and 50 (the reader is urged to bear in mind that individual differences must be taken into account, since some highly intelligent elderly do in fact outperform younger persons).

What are the bases of arguments supporting a decline or no decline in intelligence? If one deemphasizes the importance of speed and perceptual motor skills, then the evidence for a decline is substantially attenuated (Green, 1969, for example, who refers to an observed decline in the performance scale as a function of nonintellectual factors and states that this scale is not suited for research between ages). If, however, these perceptual motor functions are deemed significant in measures of intelligence, then one interprets the findings as consistent with the decline hypothesis (Botwinick & Storandt, 1973, for example). These latter investigators submit that a slowing down of response rates is a function of aging and is therefore properly construed as a part of ability and capacity. Botwinick refers to studies in which untimed scoring was used with two speed WAIS subtests and, although the significance of the differences between the age groups was reduced, the older groups still did not perform to the high level of the younger groups (despite the fact that the older group benefited by the extra time). He concludes that, although the classic aging pattern can be reduced somewhat, the performance component, which shows invariant decline, is a function of intellectual factors.

Botwinick (1977) reports on studies that have identified a *General Ability*, in which cross-sectional studies have not found age to be a significant factor in overall intelligence. Level of education, on the other hand, is observed as the variable accounting for a significant portion of the variance in general intellectual ability. In any case, Botwinick aptly suggests that the critical unanswered question concerns how important test abilities are in the real life situations of the elderly.

Longitudinal Studies

A sampling problem is but one of the factors confounding interpretations of data from cross-sectional and longitudinal approaches to the study of the stability of intelligence. For example, in a cross-sectional study random sampling is related to significant age differences, whereas subjects matched for educational background yield no significant differences in test performance. The longitudinal method (as well as the cross-sectional method) is beset by the problem of subject dropout (for a variety of reasons, a major one of which is health status); it is observed that, from initial test time to subsequent test time, only selected individuals participate, these being the intellectually brighter, thus yielding results not generalizable to the general population (i.e., the less capable are not part of the second testing, thus raising the mean performance scores). For example, in a 10-year study Eisdorfer and Wilkie (1973) report a significant loss of subjects as follows: 72% of subjects in the lowest IQ group, 51.4% in the middle IQ group, and 36.8% in the high IQ group. As Riegel, Riegel, and Meyer (1967) so aptly submit, the selective droppping out of subjects affects the trend of scores, since successive age samples in cross-sectional and longitudinal studies are skewed due to an increasing number of superior subjects. There are several reasons for this phenomenon of dropping out, one of which is referred to as "terminal drop," when it is observed that the less able apparently die before those who function better intellectually. Riegel and Riegel (1972) point out that those whose performance on cognitive tasks reflects substantial change will probably be dead within a short period of time (e.g., up to within 4–5 years); that is, a significant decrement in the expression of intellectual ability is consistently observed just prior to death. Troll, Saltz, and Dunin-Markiewicz (1976) report that dropouts in their study had lower original test scores than those in the follow-up group and that more deterioration in functional health status characterized the dropout group. Also, there is the problem of practice effects from repeated testing. All in all, cross-sectional studies tend to maximize age differences, whereas longitudinal studies tend to minimize differences, leading at times to contradictory conclusions.

Specifically, a number of cross-sectional studies find a performance peak at about twenty or thirty years, with a marked decline thereafter (Horn & Cattell, 1966). Longitudinal studies, however, find little or no decline and, in some cases, performance increments into the 50s (Bayley & Oden, 1955; Eisdorfer, 1963; Owens, 1966). A number of cross-sectional and longitudinal studies indicate a significant decline in spatial abilities, with a lesser decrement found in the older male subject (Cohen, 1977). However, Cohen suggests that the evidence is equivocal and urges further research, despite the difficulties inherent in the measurement of spatio-visual performance.

A third approach presumably obviates the problem of random sampling and the effects of environmental change for cohorts by utilizing a sequential analysis of performance scores from at least two cross-sectional studies. The design can be carried out either through a random sample of the original test group at selected points in time or by obtaining repeated performance scores of all those participants from the original testing (Schaie & Strother, 1968). Schaie and La-Bouvie-Vief (1974) conducted a 14-year cross-sequential study and reported an age decrement for the cross-sectional part of the study. However, longitudinal analysis failed to show age related or ontogenetic decline. The data were interpreted as indicating a slowing down of sensory output but were not regarded as evidence for invariant neurological deficit. These authors suggested therefore that, compared to their cohorts, cognitive performance is stable notwithstanding their poorer performance relative to their younger counterparts.

The longitudinal studies find little or no decrement up to around age 50, specifically not in the verbal skills already in the elderly's repertoire and in information usage. Some decline in speeded performance-like tests is observed, as by Jarvik and Blum (1971), who suggest that decrement on speeded psychomotor tasks is a predictable phenomenon of aging.

Botwinick (1977) discusses at length a cross-sequential analysis of data covering a 14 year span and also a comparative analysis of age decline in primary mental abilities scores. In the main, he concludes that the "difference between longitudinal and cross-sectional age patterns is more quantitative than qualitative [p. 598]."

Some studies indicate performance increments into the 70s for verbally loaded tests, with some decrement in visual motor functions at that advanced age. The important factor, as reported in Botwinick (1977), is the significance of difference between generations. The cohorts of 1913 outperformed those born in 1906, which is hypothesized as being a function of educational background (those born in 1913 having had more education) and not of age decline.

Finally, studies indicate that the intellectually bright tend to perform well across the life-span; however, one cannot accurately predict the magnitude of age decline in later years from performance in early young years. Expressed differently, those who were intellectually bright in youth tend to improve in cognitive performance tasks, to show decline later (than the average), and to decline at a slower rate.

In short, performance in verbal tasks maintains stability, all things being equal, such as health status, while performance on speeded tests shows a steady decline, that is, the classic aging pattern. Some studies report a decline on perceptual-motor speeded tasks beginning betwen the ages of 18 and 40, with concurrent increments in verbal performance, whereas other studies show increments on both verbal and speeded tests between 16 and 36 years, although the verbal gains were somewhat more consistent and of greater magnitude. Still other studies show gains in verbal scores into the 80s and 90s albeit speeded tests show decrement.

Birren (1973) reiterates the question, "How do man's intellectual abilities mature and age?" To the extent that researchers derive the multiplicity of answers to that question through vigorous experimentation and behavioral analysis, psychologists and educators can minimize cognitive decrements while at the same time maximizing adaptive behavior, which, as I said earlier, will lead to the betterment both of the individual and of the culture.

Summary and Evaluation

The literature of aging and intelligence abounds with contradictory evidence on the nature of intellectual variability (or stability). Some investigators have argued, for example, that decrement observed in the later years is not indicative of a gradual decline but rather is a symptomatic decline just prior to death, regardless of age. Some suggest that since reported deficits can be modified through intervention, these decrements are a function of factors other than intellectual ones. Interpretations of data from various approaches to testing are largely the bases of contradiction. Cross-sectional studies seem to confound interindividual differences with generational differences. Longitudinal studies seem to confound historical change with interindividual variability in given time periods. There is obviously sampling bias present in both approaches, although the effects are expressed differently. Cross and time sequential studies have been suggested to neutralize the problems associated with the foregoing approaches, since they purport to study independently the effects of aging, cohort (generational) differences, and time (historical-cultural) differences. It would appear highly improbable that any of these approaches would completely obviate the sampling difficulties which serve to dilute the inferences suggested for observed variability between and within groups.

In other words, it is almost inconceivable that an investigator can arrange a truly representative sample at each age or from each generation. In addition, there are other ambiguities surrounding the usage of statistical analyses (analysis of variance, for example) on these data, when the assumptions for their use are questionable. I am not suggesting, however, that research on aging and intelligence be discontinued because our designs and models are relatively imperfect. On the contrary, I am suggesting continued study along with the realization that our conclusions regarding the significance of differences are qualifiably tentative.

Contingent upon one's definition of intelligence, data are interpreted to indicate a decline in some intellectual skills or no significant decline in general intelligence over the years. The Wechsler studies provide compelling evidence for different abilities varying in their expression through the years. The theory of fluid and crystallized intelligence has had a profound influence on the thinking of gerontologists. This theory essentially posits that general intelligence consists of fluid capacities, for which there is some probability of decrement with age, and of crystallized abilities, for which there is some probability of increment with age (contingent upon a healthy central nervous system). Crystallized abilities are observed to improve with continued education and other experiences of a problem solving nature, while fluid abilities are subject to neurological degeneration and are therefore subject to decline.

I am inclined to believe that as one's age increases, the probability of decline in some intellectual skills also increases, compared to one's earlier performance and compared to one's younger counterpart. There are wide individual differences both in the skills that show decline and in the rate at which they decline, if indeed there is a significant decline.

LEARNING AND INTELLIGENCE [2]

Many times in the literature one sees references to intelligence as learning ability; however, empirical evidence for such a relationship is indeed lacking (Scarr-Salapatek, 1977). As we have seen, many investigators view both learning and intelligence as multivariate entities; that is, more than one ability is tapped in a general intelligence test, and, moreover, they have diverse relationships to biological and psychosocial factors.

Doubtless learning and intelligence are related, albeit in a deeply ambiguous way since, for one thing, performance on an intelligence test is a function of certain skills and information acquired through experience (in addition to influences from biological-maturational mechanisms). Similarly, age differences in performance tasks, all factors being equal, provide us with a measure of learning ability. In short, intelligence tests require that one either recall what one has learned in the past or that one use past learning to solve novel problems.

The notion of learning ability is inferred from performance in learning performance tasks, just as intelligence is inferred from data taken from psychometric instruments. In construing a definition of learning ability, it is useful to point to individual differences in rate or speed of learning when all experimental and experiential factors have been controlled. Under well controlled experimental conditions and in a wide variety of tasks, individual differences in rate of learning are observed. These differences are interpreted as a function of differences in learning ability. I am not suggesting, however, that there is an isomorphic relationship between learning ability and kind of task. On the contrary, these rates are also a function of maturational factors and experience with similar tasks. The amount of variance due to these latter factors should vary according to the kind of performance task given. (Whether the aforementioned differences are due to genetic or environmental factors would seem to be of less importance than whether environmental contingencies can be arranged to neutralize their extent.)

As discussed earlier, learning rates are related to registration and coding strategies, rehearsal, organization, etc. Individual differences in these operations or response systems could also be a function of differences in biological factors operating in conjunction with organismic variables and total learning experiences. What we have then is an enormously complex interaction between learning and intelligence, which may or may not be disentangled to everyone's satisfaction. Given that a relationship of learning performance tasks to conventional ability systems exists, we are still faced with the problem that the abilities have not been linked, in a direct manner, to antecedent conditions and mechanisms.

[2]Baltes and LaBouvie (1973) provide a comprehensive discussion of the nature of this relationship.

Roberts (1968–1969) published a review of the literature related to the problem of abilities and learning, the conclusions of which I shall simply summarize. With regard to the relationship of aptitudes and learning task performance, the studies discussed indicate that: (a) a variety of ability and learning factors have been identified; (b) no general learning or ability factor had been identified as accounting for the variance on either all ability or all learning factors; (c) ability and learning factors are related in varying degrees; and (d) not all ability factors are related to learning factors. With regard to learning–ability relationships as a function of stage of practice: (a) Relationships appear to vary according to stage of practice; (b) A confounding of decreasing-increasing relationships occurs; and (c) The stage of practice creates additional ambiguities as to the nature of learning–ability relationships. As far as Roberts is concerned, interactions between performance in learning tasks and abilities have been empirically established, despite the fact that the locations of these interactions have not been identified.

Memory Related Factors

In order to provide more definitive information concerning the changing relationship between learning and intelligence, LaBouvie, Frohring, Baltes, and Goulet (1973) administered free recall tasks to college aged students, predicting that recall scores would be significantly related to general intellectual ability under delayed recall conditions and that memory factors would be significantly related to recall scores under immediate recall conditions. In addition, they hypothesized that during the initial phase of acquisition recall performance would be mainly a function of memory, whereas in the final phase performance would be more related to intelligence.

Results indicate that cognitive factors reliably predict the later stages of delayed recall, whereas memory factors predict well for immediate recall during the early phase of acquisition. The finding of varying relationships between measures of recall and intelligence and memory was interpreted as suggestive of "the operation of trial- and treatment-related, distinct processes, despite highly similar task demands [p. 195]." The findings are interpreted as consistent with their predictions.

Although the study has several implications from a theoretical or methodological viewpoint, I am mainly interested in the authors' suggestion that these present findings are encouraging for continued, intensive investigations of the changing relationship of learning measures to ability measures during the stages of the acquisition process.

The foregoing studies involved younger, college aged subjects; however, Hultsch, Nesselroade, and Plemons (1976) conducted a study of learning–ability relations in which 114 female subjects of age range 18 to 85 participated in multitrial free recall tasks under the learning to learn model. The learning tasks consisted of two 30-word lists, each word being exposed for 1.5 seconds, with a 4-minute interval between presentation of lists. Subjects were asked to write down the words recalled. The ability tasks consisted of eight tests that measure the full range of abilities, extending from association, memory span, and perceptual speed through reasoning ability. These tests were completed approximately a week after the learning tests.

The authors interpreted the findings as consistent with the hypothesis of differential patterns of learning–ability relations as a function of age and stage of learning process. Of particular interest is the fact that memory factors were highly related to performance for the older participants.

Finally, I should like to underscore the evidence suggesting that, in the older adult, learning and performance in cognitive tasks are related to level of intelligence. Persons with low IQ's tend to show decrement in ability to learn, whereas those of high IQ show negligible, if any, decline with age. Performance on IQ tests is directly related, to a considerable extent, to one's educational and/or informational background, which varies.

It seems entirely appropriate to assume that one learns cognitive skills according to established principles of learning. Insofar as one uses these skills on a sustained basis, decrement in performance should not be observed. Of course, the maintenance of the behavior related to these skills is contingent upon the same principles of learning (including corollary conditions of reinforcement). However, Cattell (1971) would submit that learning affects only *crystallized* intelligence but not *fluid* intelligence, since this is neurologically determined. Estes (1974), on the other hand, suggests that learning is the basis of all intelligence.

PROBLEM SOLVING

As indicated earlier, the definition of intelligence, especially that of the adult, is characterized by deep ambiguities; however, it would seem that the study of problem solving provides an understanding of the nature of intelligence, since typical general intelligence tests consist of sets of problems to be solved. Performance is measured and one's problem solving ability, relative to others, is subsequently expressed quantitatively, sometimes as an IQ.

It would appear that numerous varied problem solving skills are utilized in a testing situation, contingent upon the nature of the problem to be solved. For example, some investigators suggest that problems involving space relations or verbal concepts require skills distinct from a general problem solving skill. In any event, our concern with this topical area stems from the amount of time the aged spend in solving problems or in testing hypotheses in real life situations. Given a relationship between intelligence and problem solving, performance on laboratory problem solving tasks (which conceivably parallels the process involved outside the laboratory) is highly significant, since the performance outcome should define both one's potential to adapt and the quality of one's present adaptation to an environment. Moreover, if the quality of one's survival is inextricably linked to one's ability to solve problems (which, as stated, shares a parallel link with our concept of the relationship of problem solving to intelligence), then indeed one would view some of the elderly differently, in light of a long history of successful problem solving (i.e., considered as a major component of intelligence). Extent of training and education no doubt are related to this ability.

Rabbitt (1977) suggests that a hierarchy of cognitive stages, in the Piagetian sense, for example, is questionable in the investigation of age changes in problem solving ability, since task demands and memory factors contribute more to the variance than age itself. Specifically, instructions on experimental procedures (i.e., as to the nature of the problem to be solved), stimulus materials and the presentation apparatus, memory capacity, and the context in which the problem is presented would appear more related to the probability of the problem's solution than would age.

The distinction between concept formation or attainment and problem solving is tenuous indeed; however, one can assume that a concept must first have been learned so that it can be applied to the solution of a problem. In both a contrived and a natural situation, an individual must first perceive that a problem exists. However, that one recognizes the presence of a problem does not necessarily indicate that one can solve it, since one's ability to solve a problem is a function of a variety of factors, such as one's background of experience with similar problems, extent of education, motivation, ability to apply particular strategies, etc.

In the typical categorization task, subjects need to learn a rule through which complex stimuli are classified according to specific properties or attributes from which their meaning in the context is derived. Shape or color and their relationships to the stimuli on display may for example be the relevant features that the subject must discover in order to solve the problem or to otherwise learn the concept. Usually, subjects are informed as to whether the display of features is a positive or negative instance of the concept to be learned. No doubt one's performance in these kinds of tasks is a function of what and how much one remembers of the series of displays, varying from simple to complex, presented during the experiment. Expressed differently, performance is directly related to what is retained in memory, which of course is defined by idiosyncratic load factors.

Also, under experimental conditions, one's attention must be both focused and be held on the problem at hand. This is effected, for example, through instructions. In addition, one must at times shift attention to another aspect of the problem, which is particularly problematic for data interpretation, since the amount of control exercised by the experimenter is attenuated by instructions of a mental nature (i.e., by self-instructions).

Finally, it would seem that compounding an already enormously complicated situation is the fact that an individual invents concepts and decides on strategies (and follows them) covertly. In short, an unspecified portion of the individual's mental operations is in addition to and beyond that accounted for through experimental procedures.

Higher Order Factors

Of the relatively few studies of complex mental functions found in the literature of gerontology, many indicate age related deficits in problem solving (Welford, 1958; Jerome, 1962; Young, 1966; Arenberg, 1974) and in critical thinking (Friend & Zubek, 1958). However, some studies do not find decrement; one of these was conducted by Wetherick (1964).

Wetherick (1964) designed a study to determine whether nonverbal intelligence was equivalent to problem solving ability, since the literature indicates a decline both in nonverbal intelligence and problem solving ability and the two are known to be related. Thirty-three male subjects, who were matched for nonverbal intelligence through Raven's Progressive Matrices test, were divided into three groups of mean ages 26.2, 44.7, and 64.1.

Each subject sat in front of a panel on which switches A, B, C, and D were located. Each switch could be moved to three different places on the panel. The task was to determine the correct position of the switch in order for a lamp to light when a panel button is depressed. There are 81 possible positions of the four switches. The subjects were each presented with three different problems. In the first, the subject was instructed that only one switch was relevant, in the second, that two were relevant, and in the third, that one, two, or three switches could be relevant to the solution, that is, in determining both the number and switch position. Upon pressing the panel button, the experimenter recorded the subjects' presses. Each subject had unlimited time, with a maximum of 15 trials. An instance is positive or negative, depending on whether or not the light comes on when the button is pressed. A positive instance would lead to a strategy for the problem's solution.

Results indicate no significant differences in the first problem, which all subjects resolved. In the second, the young and middle aged groups outperformed the older group, who solved the fewest problems and made more noninformative instances. In the third problem, which was the most difficult, there were no significant differences both in number of correct solutions and in noninformative instances; that is, the performance of the old group was qualitatively better than that of the other groups. Wetherick attributes this to learning from their experience in problem two (i.e., learning how to avoid noninformative instances).

The author suggests that the decrements found in earlier studies were a function of the subjects' not being matched on nonverbal intelligence. Moreover, the brighter elderly person seems to hold his ability to profit from experience despite the presumed loss of ability to perform well on nonverbal measures of intelligence.

Rabbitt (1965) presented card sorting tasks to old and young subjects and reported that sorting times varied as a function of the number of irrelevant cues and by the variations of irrelevant symbols on visual display. The old were found to take longer to discriminate (process) between important and unimportant letters in tasks in which they searched for two or eight letters among varying numbers of unimportant letters. Results indicate that older subjects sample smaller sets or groups (i.e., dividing them into subclasses) of letters than the younger subjects, which he assumed is due to a perceptual acuity deficit increasing with age. Although Wetherick (1964) used a different task, he reports no tendency for his older subjects to accumulate redundant (irrelevant) information, a finding which is not unrelated to Rabbitt's conclusion.

Young (1966) reported that, in logical analysis problems, older subjects demonstrated difficulty partially because of their inability to ignore unimportant information and because of memory decrement; however, the most significant finding was their apparent inability to learn or to apply a solution strategy in the application of which they received instructions.

Friend and Zubek (1958) conducted a study in which 484 volunteer subjects of mainly professional, semiprofessional, and student status and ranging in age from 12 to 80 years were given tests of critical thinking. The test consisted of 99 questions, virtually all of which involved problems of an everyday or practical nature; no time limit was required. Within this context, the test measured five subabilities of critical thinking described as inference, recognition of assumptions, deduction, interpretation, and evaluation of arguments. Results indicate that critical thinking, as defined by a composite of five subabilities, develops rapidly shortly after the teen years, peaks out in the mid-20s, and stabilizes through the mid-30s, at which point a steady decline through the 70s and 80s is observed.

These investigators point out that the shape of the curves for critical thinking ability is similar to that derived from tests of general intelligence, such as the early Wechsler scales. The most obvious difference is that critical thinking develops later and declines later than general intelligence, according to these data. Friend and Zubek interpreted these findings of poorer performance for the elderly subjects as a function of the elderly's lowered objectivity in responding to emotionally laden questions, such as those involving politics, and of their inflexibility as shown by their tendency to answer questions in absolutes, such as true or false, rather than to consider other alternatives.

By way of summary, the sparse literature in problem solving reflects decline, with age, in such tasks as logical reasoning and in tasks requiring analysis and synthesis. Whether this reported decrement is a function of rigidity or loss of cognitive ability is questionable. However, there is compelling evidence that seems to indicate that the elderly's problem solving difficulties are related to certain inefficiencies in organizing complex material and in discriminating among task stimuli, as well as to failure to respond (as discussed in this and earlier chapters). Additionally, Canestrari (1967) suggests that the aged suffer a loss in ability to abstract and in short term memory, both of which may be related to deterioration in the central nervous system. Wetherick (1975) submits that the elderly's difficulties with tasks requiring use of higher mental functions is related to limited short term memory ability, especially for unfamiliar material. Under contrived problem solving conditions, the elderly use more time relative to younger groups, and, when additional time is allotted, performance decrement is still observed.

Concept Attainment

Wetherick (1966) conducted three experiments in which subjects were to select, under no time limit, one letter or a pair of letters (i.e., the concept) that was present in all positive instances but not in any negative instance. Thirty male subjects matched for nonverbal intelligence were divided into three groups of age ranges 21–30, 42–49, and 60–70 for Experiment I. The problems were constructed so that three types of errors could be distinguished. A Type I error indicates that the subject used the wrong strategy. In Type II, the subject did not utilize all the instances given. In Type III, the subject reversed the sign of instances used and selected the letter or pair found in at least one negative instance but not in any positive instance.

Results from Experiment I indicate no differences in number of problems solved; however, the old group made many more Type I errors than the other two groups, whose performance was virtually identical on all three types of errors.

Five groups of subjects matched for nonverbal intelligence and divided into 10 year intervals from ages 20 to 69 served in Experiment II. Results indicate no significant differences in number of problems solved correctly, but again the incidence of Type I error was observed to increase significantly with age. In a concept attainment problem, memory of whether or not instances had already been used is required; however, when this memory requirement is eliminated, as was done in Experiment II, the incidence of errors decreased significantly.

In Experiment III, 42 subjects, not matched, were divided into three groups of age ranges 20–35, 40–55, and 60–75. Results indicate a pattern similar to those of Experiments I and II in the number of correct solutions and the incidence of error type.

Wetherick interpreted the apparent failure of the older subjects to discriminate mixed instances from positive as a factor related to the rigidity often observed in the elderly; however, Wetherick suggests that a performance decrement in problem solving by the elderly is not a function of rigidity per se, and he points to the findings of Experiment II, in which the Type I error was neutralized. In a series of further studies, Wetherick (1975) suggests that performance decrements for the aged in tasks involving higher mental operations are a partial function of their somewhat restricted short term memory ability, particularly for novel material.

Kesler, Denney, and Whitely (1976) report a significant relationship between education and problem solving ability and also state that age differences are negligible when subjects are matched for nonverbal intelligence, which is consistent with Wetherick (1964). However, they aptly suggested that before comparisons with other studies dealing with higher mental operations are made, researchers should take into account level of education, occupation, and other characteristics of the subjects used in the studies.

MODIFICATION THROUGH INTERVENTION

Throughout this book I have discussed instances of improved performance through reduction of task demands or through manipulation of time intervals. Recently, some researchers have utilized cumulative learning and operant conditioning principles in a direct intervention approach to the modification of decrements observed in the cognitive behavior of the elderly.

The cumulative learning model suggests that the learning of anything proceeds from first acquiring simple associationistic, S-R connections as prerequisite steps to the acquisition of complex concepts; that is, concepts would be learned to the extent that simpler associations, arranged in a hierarchy, were first learned (Gagne, 1977). For example, a specific technique utilizing hierarchical principles is found in the use of a programmed learning instrument, in which acquisition of a higher order skill is contingent upon acquisition of a lower order skill (i.e., similar to shaping in the operant model).

The operant model stresses the environment as the major determinant of behavior, notwithstanding an individual's contribution to the interaction (Skinner, 1969). Operant conditioning focuses on response rate or frequency and posits that response rate is a function of a specific reinforcement contingency, which of course means that the rate can be modified by altering contingencies. Within a teaching–learning context, contingencies of reinforcement are construed as characterized by an occasion upon which behavior is emitted, the observed behavior itself, and the consequences of the behavior. A reinforcement is a specific type of consequence.

The technique to effect change involves identification of the target behavior to be conditioned and specification of the rate at which this particular behavior has been emitted prior to the experiment; that is, in establishing a baseline frequency. Then a reinforcer, such as positive feedback, praise, or money must be specified for the specific target behavior. This operation can be particularly problematic, since reinforcers may or may not have wide applicability, especially in the aged. Getting the reinforcer is then made contingent upon emitting the desired or appropriate behavior, which in turn comes under the control of the reinforcer and of the reinforcement contingency itself, which is further defined by the schedule under which the reinforcer is made available. As I stated earlier, there is a virtual infinity of scheduling combinations. The effect is that the behavior reinforced is observed to occur more frequently. Moreover, the effects of increased behavior generalize to similar environmental situations.

The operant model focuses on current environmental contingencies in the modification and maintenance of behavior, although the model recognizes the role of an individual's reinforcement history. Emphasis is simply placed on the immediate environment and the antecedent conditions which will be most significant in controlling (and predicting) behavior, independent of historical events presumably related to the target behavior. The impact of environment on the elderly was amply discussed in Chapter 1.

Higher Order Skills

Wetherick (1966) and Arenberg (1968) improved the performance of the elderly through a reduction in task demands; however, a number of other investigators have observed performance increments through direct intervention strategies, utilizing cumulative learning and operant conditioning principles in conjunction with training procedures (Crovitz, 1966; Denney, 1974; Sanders, Sterns, Smith, & Sanders, 1975; Hornblum & Overton, 1976; Sanders, Sanders, Mayes, & Sielski, 1976). These investigators suggest that the difficulties encountered by the elderly in tasks involving higher mental operations are significantly related to non-neural (fixed) factors, such as limited background of educational and cultural experiences, along with present environmental limitations.

Denney (1974) found that a group of elderly subjects benefited from a modeling strategy utilized to enhance similarity grouping of geometric stimuli rather than classify them by the less efficient design grouping. Meichenbaum (1974) suggests that use of self-instructional strategies to compensate for age related deficits in problem solving. With this technique, the subject would verbalize instructions related to heuristic processes which lead to the solution of problems. Sanders, Sterns, *et al.* (1975) used cumulative learning principles in conjunction with operant procedures under programmed learning conditions to reduce decrement in difficult concept attainment tasks. Hornblum and Overton

(1976) utilized verbal feedback contingencies to induce significant improvement in area and volume conservation tasks and suggested that the feedback, in addition to simply reinforcing specific responses, activated competence based strategies already present in the older person's repertoire. Sanders *et al.* (1976) used training procedures derived from cumulative learning and operant principles and demonstrated performance increments in conjunctive concept identification.

Paralleling the thrust of the foregoing studies, Sanders *et al.* (1975) demonstrated that the performance of subjects with a mean age of 71 on concept identification tasks was significantly improved through special training procedures which included principles of the operant model in conjunction with a programmed learning sequence comparable to operant shaping. These investigators suggested that the observed performance increments are largely a function of the training procedure itself, such as the sequencing of tasks, which resulted in the development of generalizable solution strategies. They also pointed out that subjects who participated in the reinforced training procedures expressed "feelings of intrinsic reinforcement and increased self-confidence because of the frequent successes they achieved during training [p. 828]," all of which is related to performance increments. The data of this study can be interpreted as strong support for the use of programmed learning techniques in the training of older persons. Extending the interpretations of these data further, Sanders *et al.* (1976) suggest that for highly complex cognitive tasks that require, for example, strong inference, the older adults' self-generated solution strategies may not be sufficient, and, therefore, training in task-specific strategies may be necessary.

In short, these studies more than adequately demonstrate that if the reported cognitive decline is viewed as a function of performance variables and not as an irreversible deficit linked to biological mechanisms, then modification of age differences can be effected through training in the skills demanded by the tasks. When external aids such as instructions for self-pacing, unrestricted time limits, and mediational devices are provided and when prior rehearsal of task demands are encouraged, significant increments in performance are observed. Moreover, since the effects of the training and intervention procedures are qualifiably generalizable, it would appear that higher order mental operations are under the control of environmental contingencies and consequences.

Other Factors Influencing Performance

LaBouvie-Vief, Hoyer, Baltes, and Baltes (1974), Schultz and Hoyer (1976), and LaBouvie-Vief (1976) have taken a strong position against the stability model of aging (such as that implied in the fluid–crystallized notion of intelligence), which posits that intellectual functioning is an immutable consequence of biological aging, which in turn is related to a widely held view that cognitive deficits are not modifiable, in any substantive sense, through manipulative-intervention procedures. These investigators are not rejecting the evidence of intellectual decline in the advanced years; instead, they argue for plasticity in cognitive performance, pointing to environmental–situational factors as the basis for change. For the analysis of age related behavior they propose an operant frame of reference in which intellectual performance is linked to operant response systems that are under the control of environmental contingencies.

Response Speed

In standard behavioral terminology, Hoyer, LaBouvie, and Baltes (1973) selected response speed as the target behavior of their study. Contrary to the assumption that speed of response deficits in the aged are a function of central nervous system changes, reflecting loss of brain cells, for example (Birren, 1959, 1964; Welford, 1965), these investigators hypothesized that speed of response decrements observed in the elderly are a function of inadequate, differential practice and schedules of reinforcement found in their environment. In this study, 32 female subjects of mean age 70 were first pretested on 11 cognitive and speed factors and were then divided into control, nonreinforced (no feedback), and reinforced practice (positive reinforcement in the form of a light, coming on when they worked faster than baseline time, and 5¢ each time the light flashed) groups. The training of speed involved three tasks called *cancellation,* in which subjects were instructed to cancel out all a's in letter strings; *marking,* in which subjects transferred symbols from one sheet to an appropriate space on another sheet; and *writing,* in which subjects copied four letter words.

Results indicate that the performance of the reinforced group was superior to that of the nonreinforced practice group. Another aspect of this pretest–posttest study was to determine if the performance increments (i.e., the increased speed) would transfer to performance on cognitive and perceptual speed tests. No significant differences were found here. The authors interpreted this as most likely related to insufficient training time and not enough training tasks. High retest gains were taken as evidence that the elderly simply lack exposure to testing conditions, relative to younger persons.

These authors urge the use of the operant model in investigations of performance plasticity in the aged, which for one thing would tend to increase the optimism regarding the nature of age related changes and potential. In a later study, Bellucci and Hoyer (1975) demonstrated performance increments in response speed, self-reinforcement, and enhanced self-evaluation as a function of positive noncontingent feedback (that could conceivably be related to the reduction of anxiety produced by learning task situations). Baltes and Barton (1977) report that cognitive feedback and token reinforcement are related to significant increases in response speed; however, transfer effects to intelligence test performance were negligible.

Cognitive Strategy

Viewing intellectual performance decrements in the aged as a function of environmental-experiential factors rather than of biological ones, LaBouvie-Vief and Gonda (1976) conducted a study in which elderly subjects received training in inductive reasoning (a skill which is closely related to the operations of fluid intelligence) problems. Specifically, the training was directed toward improving the elderly's self-instructional strategies, which have been characterized as inefficient.

Results indicate both performance increments and transfer, which were observed to hold for approximately 2 weeks (which is not to imply that the effects were not sustained longer than 2 weeks). The authors point out that the presence of any training effects can be interpreted as compelling evidence for plasticity in adult intelligence and against the notion of an irreversible deficit.

Cautiousness

That cautiousness and conservatism are concomitants of the aging process has been reported in the literature a number of times (Kuhlen, 1959; Botwinick, 1966), along with the suggestion that age differences are a partial function of this construct in the performance of verbal learning tasks (Eisdorfer, 1965) and memory tasks (Eysenck, 1975). Recently, however, investigators have taken that assumption to task by demonstrating that age differences in risk taking behaviors are modifiable through manipulative strategies related to task variables (Birkhill & Schaie, 1975; Okun & DiVesta, 1976; Okun, 1976; Okun & Elias, 1977). There are a variety of theoretical frameworks of which the reader is encouraged to read that describe the nature of cautiousness (Okun, 1976) and the relationship of rigidity to cautiousness (Botwinick, 1973).

Okun and Elias (1977) demonstrated that older subjects are not more cautious than their younger counterparts when degree of risk taking was varied in conjunction with a monetary payoff, that is, when the size of the payoff varied with the size of the risk. Results indicate that risk taking is significantly related to payoff contingencies. The monetary incentive conceivably could have affected the subjects' motivation in the sense that interest in the task, which may have been otherwise unimportant, was increased (I discussed this somewhat ambiguous relationship within a verbal learning context in Chapter 2). Moreover, the incentive may have served to channel attention to the task; however, the differential effects of attention shifts related to the probability of getting a reward or, in this instance, to risk taking (i.e., to probability of success) seem to be hopelessly confounded.

In any case, Birkhill and Schaie (1975) indicate that older subjects will increase their risk taking behavior on cognitive measures under differential incentive conditions. Specifically, they found that subjects under low risk conditions realized performance increments on intelligence measures when they had the option of responding or not responding to test items (I should point out that many of the studies reporting age differences in cautiousness used the choice dilemma instrument as the measuring tool).

Summary and Evaluation

It would appear paramount in our interpretations of data derived from adult testing studies that we recognize state variables (in spite of their highly inferential nature) as contributing an unspecified portion of the variance in performance scores on tasks which presumably measure cognitive skills. These variables include such things as the testee's attitude toward being tested; that is, performance emitted by a volunteer should differ from that of one who served as a subject in a research project conducted at an institution, partially because of predisposition and not ability. Undoubtedly, motivational variables of an infinite variety serve as determinants in all kinds of behavior. Anxiety, for example, is a manipulable variable, the reduction of which leads to performance increments in both young and old.

Cautiousness and forms of rigidity (however defined) would seem better conceptualized as having experiential bases, subject to manipulation and modification.

In all of our learning–performance or intelligence tests, the question of relevance is pervasive. Sorting cards and assembling blocks under timed conditions might be construed, by the older person, as irrelevant to intelligent or otherwise adaptive behavior.

Fatigue, whether or not it is viewed as ability extraneous, is a critical variable affecting the performance of older persons (or young persons in power tests, for example).

Finally, health status takes on singular importance when the performance of older subjects in relatively poor health is compared to that of younger age groups or like age groups who are in relatively better health. No doubt some older persons do not perceive and retrieve informational stimuli to their potential or capacity because of central nervous system dysfunctions and not because of age. In other words, it appears highly probable that performance decrements suggested as due to age were a function of physiological inefficiencies.

CONCLUDING REMARKS

We have examined both the evidence in support of the plasticity of intelligence in adulthood and the evidence pointing to universal, systematic decrement in the later years. Variance in intellectual performance has on the one hand been accounted for by biological-maturational factors and on the other by environmental contingencies. The limitations associated with the major approaches to the investigation of aging and intelligence lead one to believe that the enormous complexities involved in age related interactions are hopelessly confounded. However, I would simply urge educational gerontologists to direct (or shift) their research priorites to environmental factors which lend themselves to manipulation, through some intervention strategy, for example. I suggest this simply because of the evidence pointing to experiential–situational variables as determinants of the elderly's difficulties in expressing performance on cognitive skill tasks; that is, age differences are observed to decrease when time restrictions are eliminated and when mediational instructions and reinforcement contingencies are provided.

It is generally agreed that the characteristic environment of the elderly is virtually void of intellectual stimulation. It would seem that both formal and informal educational programs are viable targets for future research designs, since there is little doubt that the elderly profit from the kinds of experience provided through these media.

REFERENCES

ARENBERG, D. Concept problem solving in young and old adults. *Journal of Gerontology,* 1968, *23,* 279–282.

ARENBERG, D. A longitudinal study of problem solving in adults. *Journal of Gerontology,* 1974, *29,* 650–658.

BALTES, M. M., & BARTON, E. M. New approaches toward aging: A case for the operant model. *Educational Gerontology,* 1977, *2,* 383–405.

BALTES, P. B., & LABOUVIE, G. V. Adult development of intellectual performance: Description, explanation and modification. In C. Eisdorfer & M. P. Lawton (Eds.), *The psychology of adult development and aging.* Washington, D.C.: American Psychological Association, 1973.

BAYLEY, N., & ODEN, M. H. The maintenance of intellectual ability in gifted adults. *Journal of Gerontology,* 1955, *10,* 91–107.

BELLUCCI, G., & HOYER, W. J. Feedback effects on the performance and self-reinforcing behavior of elderly and young adult women. *Journal of Gerontology,* 1975, *30*(4), 456–460.

BIRKHILL, W. R., & SCHAIE, K. W. The effect of differential reinforcement of cautiousness in intellectual performance among the elderly. *Journal of Gerontology,* 1975, *30*(5), 578–583.

BIRREN, J. E. In J. E. Birren, *Handbook of aging and the individual.* Chicago: University of Chicago Press, 1959.

BIRREN, J. E. *The psychology of aging.* Englewood Cliffs, N. J.: Prentice-Hall, 1964.

BIRREN, J. E. A summary: Prospects and problems of research on the longitudinal development of man's intellectual capacities throughout life. In L. F. Jarvik, C. Eisdorfer, & J. E. Blum (Eds.), *Intellectual functioning in adults.* New York: Springer, 1973.

BOTWINICK, J. Cautiousness in advanced age. *Journal of Gerontology*, 1966, *21*, 347-355.

BOTWINICK, J. *Cognitive processes in maturity and old age*. New York: Springer, 1967.

BOTWINICK, J. *Aging and behavior: A comprehensive integration of research findings*. New York: Springer, 1973.

BOTWINICK, J. Intellectual abilities. In J. E. Birren & K. W. Schaie (Eds.), *Handbook of the psychology of aging*. New York: Van Nostrand Reinhold, 1977.

BOTWINICK, J., & STORANDT, M. Speed functions, vocabulary ability and age. *Perceptual Motor Skills*, 1973, *36*, 1123-1128.

CANESTRARI, R. E. Research in learning. *The Gerontologist*, 1967, 7(2,Pt.2), 61-66.

CATTELL, R. B. The theory of fluid and crystallized intelligence: A critical experiment. *Journal of Educational Psychology*, 1963, *54*, 1-22.

CATTELL, R. B. *Abilities: Their structure, growth, and action*. Boston: Houghton-Mifflin, 1971.

COHEN, D., & BEHAVIORAL BIOLOGY UNIT. Sex differences in spatial performance in the elderly: A review of the literature and suggestions for research. *Educational Gerontology: An International Quarterly*, 1977, *2*, 59-69.

CROVITZ, E. Reversing a learning deficit in the aged. *Journal of Gerontology*, 1966, *21*, 236-238.

DENNEY, N. W. Classification abilities in the elderly. *Journal of Gerontology*, 1974, *29*, 309-314.

EISDORFER, C. The WAIS performance of the aged: A retest evaluation. *Journal of Gerontology*, 1963, *18*, 169-172.

EISDORFER, C. Verbal learning and response time in the aged. *Journal of Genetic Psychology*, 1965, *107*, 15-22.

EISDORFER, C., & WILKIE, F. Intellectual changes with advancing age. In L. F. Jarvik, C. Eisdorfer, & J. E. Blum (Eds.), *Intellectual functioning in adults, psychological and biological influences*. New York: Springer, 1973.

ESTES, W. K. Learning theory and intelligence. *American Psychologist*, 1974, *29*, 740-749.

EYSENCK, M. Retrieval from semantic memory as a function of age. *Journal of Gerontology*, 1975, *30*, 174-180.

FRIEND, C. M., & ZUBEK, J. P. The effects of age on critical thinking ability. *Journal of Gerontology*, 1958, *13*, 407-413.

FURRY, C. A., & BALTES. The effect of age differences in ability-extraneous performance variables on the assessment of intelligence in children, adults, and the elderly. *Journal of Gerontology*, 1973, *28*, 73-80.

GAGNE, R. M. *The conditions of learning*, Third edition. New York: Holt, Rinehart and Winston, 1977.

GRANICK, S., & FRIEDMAN, A. S. Educational experience and maintenance of intellectual functioning by the aged: An overview. In L. F. Jarvik, C. Eisdorfer, & J. E. Blum (Eds.), *Intellectual functioning in adults*. New York: Springer, 1973.

GREEN, R. F. Age intelligence relationship between ages sixteen and sixty-four: A rising trend. *Developmental Psychology*, 1969, *1*, 618-627.

HORN, J. L., & CATTELL, R. B. Age differences in primary mental ability factors. *Journal of Gerontology*, 1966, *21*, 210-220.

HORN, J. L., & CATTELL, R. B. Age differences in fluid and crystallized intelligence. *Acta Psychologica*, 1967, *26*, 107-129.

HORNBLUM, J. N., & OVERTON, W. F. Area and volume conservation among the elderly: Assessment and training. *Developmental Psychology, 1976, 12*(1), 68–74.

HOYER, W. J., LABOUVIE, G. V., & BALTES, P. B. Modification of response speed deficits and intellectual performance in the elderly. *Human Development,* 1973, *16,* 233–242.

HULTSCH, D. F., NESSELROADE, J. R., & PLEMONS, J. K. Learning ability relations in adulthood. *Human Development,* 1976, *19,* 234–247.

JARVIK, L. F., & BLUM, J. E. Cognitive declines as predictors of mortality in twin pairs: A twenty-year longitudinal study of aging. In E. Palmore & F. C. Jeffers (Eds.), *Prediction of life span.* Boston: Heath, 1971.

JEROME, E. A. Decay of heuristic processes in the aged. In C. Tibbitts & W. Donahue (Eds.), *Social and psychological aspects of aging.* New York: Columbia University Press, 1962.

KESLER, M. S., DENNEY, N. W., & WHITELY, S. E. Factors influencing problem solving in middle aged and elderly adults. *Human Development,* 1976, *19,* 310-320.

KUHLEN, R. G. Aging and life adjustment. In J. E. Birren (Ed.), *Handbook of aging and the individual: Psychological and social aspects.* Chicago: University of Chicago Press, 1959.

LABOUVIE, G. V., FROHRING, W. R., BALTES, P. B., & GOULET, L. R. Changing relationship between recall performance and abilities as a function of learning and timing of recall. *Journal of Educational Psychology,* 1973, *64*(2), 191–198.

LABOUVIE, V. G. V., HOYER, W. J., BALTES, M. M., & BALTES, P. B. Operant analysis of intellectual behavior in old age. *Human Development,* 1974, *17,* 259–272.

LABOUVIE-VIEF, G. Toward optimizing cognitive competence in later life. *Educational Gerontology: An International Quarterly,* 1967, *1,* 75–92.

LABOUVIE-VIEF, G., & GONDA, J. N. Cognitive strategy training and intellectual performance in the elderly. *Journal of Gerontology,* 1976, *31,* 327–331.

MEICHENBAUM, D. Self-instructional strategy training: A cognitive prothesis for the aged. *Human Development,* 1974, *17,* 273-280.

OKUN, M. A. Adult age and cautiousness in decision: A review of the literature. *Human Development,* 1976, *19,* 220–233.

OKUN, M., & DIVESTA, F. J. Cautiousness in adulthood as a function of age and instructions. *Journal of Gerontology,* 1976, *31*(5), 571–576.

OKUN, M. A., & ELIAS, C. S. Cautiousness in adulthood as a function of age and payoff structure, *Journal of Gerontology,* 1977, *32*(4), 451–455.

OWENS, W. A. Age and mental abilities: A second adult follow up. *Journal of Educational Psychology,* 1966, *57,* 311–325.

RABBITT, P. M. A. An age decrement in the ability to ignore irrelevant information. *Journal of Gerontology,* 1965, *20,* 233–238.

RABBITT, P. Changes in problem solving ability in old age. In J. E. Birren & K. W. Schaie (Eds.), *Handbook of the psychology of aging.* New York: Van Nostrand Reinhold, 1977.

RIEGEL, K. F., & RIEGEL, R. M. Development, drop and death. *Developmental Psychology,* 1972, *6,* 306–319.

RIEGEL, K. F., RIEGEL, R. M., & MEYER, G. Socio-psychological factors of aging: A cohort-sequential analysis. *Human Development,* 1967, *10,* 27-56.

ROBERTS, D. M. Abilities and learning: A brief review and discussion of empirical studies. *Journal of School Psychology,* 1968-69, *7,* 12-21.

SANDERS, J. C., STERNS, H. L., SMITH, M., & SANDERS, R. E. Modification of concept identification performance in older adults. *Developmental Psychology,* 1975, *11*(6), 824-829.

SANDERS, R. E., SANDERS, J. A., MAYES, G. J., & SIELSKI, K. A. Enhancement of conjunctive concept attainment in older adults. *Developmental Psychology,* 1976, *12*(5), 485-486.

SCARR-SALAPATEK, S. Learning intelligence and intelligence testing. In M. H. Marx & M. E. Bunch (Eds.), *Fundamentals and applications of learning.* New York: Macmillan, 1977.

SCHAIE, K. W., & LABOUVIE-VIEF, G. Generational versus ontogenetic components of change in adult cognitive behavior: A fourteen-year cross-sequential study. *Developmental Psychology,* 1974, *10,* 305-320.

SCHAIE, K. W., & STROTHER, C. R. A cross sequential study of age changes in cognitive behavior. *Psychological Bulletin,* 1968, *70,* 671-680.

SCHULTZ, N. R., & HOYER, W. J. Feedback effects on spatial egocentrism in old age. *Journal of Gerontology,* 1976, *31,* 72-75.

SKINNER, B. F. *Contingencies of reinforcement: A theoretical analysis.* New York: Appleton Century Crofts, 1969.

TROLL, L. E., SALTZ, R., & DUNIN-MARKIEWICZ, A. A seven-year follow-up of intelligence test scores of foster grandparents. *Journal of Gerontology,* 1976, *31,* 583-585.

WECHSLER, D. *The measurement and appraisal of adult intelligence,* Fourth edition. Baltimore: Williams and Wilkins, 1958.

WELFORD, A. T. *Aging and human skill.* London: Oxford University Press, 1958.

WELFORD, A. T. Performance, biological mechanism and age: A theoretical sketch. In A. T. Welford & J. E. Birren, *Behavior, aging and the nervous system.* Springfield: Thomas, 1965.

WETHERICK, N. E. A comparison of the problem solving ability of young, middle aged and old subjects. *Gerontologia,* 1964, *9,* 164-178.

WETHERICK, N. E. The inferential basis of concept attainment. *British Journal of Psychology,* 1966, *57,* 61-69.

WETHERICK, N. E. Age, short term memory capacity, and the higher mental functions. In D. B. Lumsden & R. H. Sherron (Eds.), *Experimental studies in adult learning and memory.* Washington, D.C.: Hemisphere Publications, 1975.

YOUNG, M. L. Problem solving performance in two age groups. *Journal of Gerontology,* 1966, *21,* 505-509.

5

Education and the Older Learner

Having examined the constructs of learning, memory, and intelligence, it now seems clear that the elderly have the capacity to learn new things and to otherwise profit from experience. Indeed, the ironic factor in the present condition is that the notion of irreversible decrement is accepted mainly where it is virtually nonexistent (i.e., by a significant number of the elderly). In other words, it would appear that, as far as some investigators (and some of the elderly) are concerned, congnitive decline follows a relentless path over the years; however, one can hardly doubt that the brighter, educated elderly know (either for personal reasons or as a result of having read the literature) that they have residual potential and that their observed poor performance is a function of non-age variables, such as interest, relevancy, and a seeming multiplicity of other ability-extraneous variables beyond the slowing of sensory functions.

The current picture is characterized by compelling evidence that extent of education and prior experience are critical variables accounting for a substantial portion of the variance in age related differences; that is, there is an inverse relationship between level of education and rate of cognitive decline, in spite of the fact that education is an abstruse, loosely defined factor.

In preceding chapters, I discussed the evidence reported by a number of investigators to the effect that when such factors as speed (interpreted by some as nonintellectual) and anxiety are controlled, significant decreases in learning performance decrements are observed. And although their performance did not match the standard of those younger, significant performance increments are observed (which is not to suggest that the elderly cannot learn as well as the younger, since some studies show that individual differences are great and that some elderly outperform their younger counterparts in a wide variety of tasks, which implicitly suggests that others, those who accept "decline," for example, are also capable of similar performance given the impetus and opportunity). Perhaps now we have arrived at the point where principle might be related to practice.

ADULT EDUCATION

Continuing education is a viable intervention strategy structured, in formal and informal ways, for both the prevention of imminent obsolescence and the enhancement of a storehouse of knowledge. This particular medium has been part of our sociocultural environment for many years and most likely will take on a more prominent stature in years to come, for a wide variety of reasons.

Given the evidence that older people have the ability to exercise cognitive skills throughout their lifetimes, all things being equal, it falls on the educator (defined in the broadest sense to include all those who would impart or otherwise explain information) to provide opportunities to close the gap in knowledge among and within generations, a situation which has been brought about by rapid technological revolution. This can be effected through well-designed educational programs administered through an adult education unit or any other teaching agency.

Role of Adult Education

The general goals of adult education can be summarized thusly: to make available opportunities for occupational, personal, and social competence, civil commitment, and self-fulfillment (Liveright, 1968). These ends are comprehensive indeed; however, the problem is found in their implementation (Peterson, 1977), since participation (which is less than desirable in general) in the activities leading to the satisfaction of these goals is restricted to a somewhat select group and not to a broadly based group as intended. Throughout this chapter I shall discuss the dynamics of this situation that are related to the elderly's needs, interests, and attitudes.

That continuing education is a necessity for successful adaptation has been established, and now the problem becomes one of the structure of adult education required to meet the needs of its clientele.

Peterson (1977) submits that a major reason for lack of participation by older persons in continuing education activities is that programs or courses have not been specifically designed for them. In particular, their needs have not been considered adequately. New programs or courses dealing with problem solving situations on the one hand to liberal arts courses on the other hand must be offered. In addition, courses which prepare the older learner for effective participation in civic or political activities in the community must be programmed for them.

Peterson also suggests that more adult educators and planners must recognize that older persons learn new concepts, etc. well into their 60s and 70s and should design coursework and activities accordingly. These designs should incorporate adequate lighting, audiovisual materials, and environmental settings which take into account the sensory, cognitive, and physical limitations of an older group of learners (Schaie, 1974; Schonfield, 1974).

Tasks of Adulthood

Havighurst (1972) defines the developmental tasks of life as those things an individual must learn in order to adapt to environmental situations so that one realizes a measure of happiness. These tasks manifest themselves at certain periods throughout one's lifetime, the successful accomplishing of which is related to happiness. Failure to learn a task inhibits one's progress toward succeeding tasks and is related to one's unhappiness. He has delineated three stages of adulthood, from which adult educators can design learning programs or experiences.

In general, the stages and accompanying representative tasks are:

Early adulthood, in which one goes through the process of selecting a mate (if one chooses to get married) so that a domestic condition can be initiated and maintained. It is also the period of progressing through the exigencies of the occupational–professional hierarchical framework.

Middle age, in which one attempts to achieve a sense of social responsibility while at the same time guiding children (if any) to the same acceptance of responsibility. In addition, one is adapting to the biological-physiological changes concomitant with the middle years.

Late adulthood (beyond age fifty), in which one is adapting to retirement and, possibly, to an increase in health problems.

It would seem apparent that one's socioeconomic status is directly related to the kinds of tasks that dominate one's condition. For example, those who are concerned mainly with survival (in the literal sense) most certainly would be confronted with different (qualitatively and quantitatively) tasks than someone from the privileged upper class.

In any case, Havighurst (1976) draws a distinction between the instrumental and expressive aspects of education, which are related to the satisfaction of these task demands. As the terms imply, the former refers to the kind of learning which is instrumental in the performance of a specific behavior such as learning to keep accounts. The latter refers to learning for the sake of learning or for the intrinsic reward of studying whatever one is studying. Obviously, the two aspects are complementary and are not mutually exclusive. Havighurst suggests that both forms of education are requisite to successful adaptation to every stage of the life cycle, with its needs and demands varying at each phase.

Although our interest lies mainly with the older learner in the later years, it appears useful to conceptualize one aspect of the learning process as lying along a continuum from childhood through the later years in a sort of interlocking form. Havighurst's categories of developmental tasks lend themselves well to this frame of reference, since competence in later tasks is construed to be a function of competence in earlier tasks (one could also express this notion in terms of antecedent-consequence conditions).

Roles and expectations are observed to change throughout the life-span, and educational programs can be designed to assist people in their interpretation and implementation of these changing personal and social roles, according to Havighurst (1976). For example, the instrumental aspect of education can satisfy the following tasks of adulthood: preparation for some profession or occupation; increasing one's competence in an occupation; rearing a family to mutual satisfaction; accepting civic and social responsibilities; and adapting to biological changes. Thus, successful adaptation is construed to be contingent upon some sort of continuing education throughout the cycles related to these tasks.

Houle (1974) defines four age periods for which viable adult education programs could be designed: (a) 20–35, during which the individual is concerned with civic, social, domestic, and employment roles, in which priorities are established and stabilized toward the end of the period; (b) 35–55, when one is concerned with the more profound implications of existence and is examining more thoroughly personal and/or social goals; (c) 55–75, when plans for the later years are being initiated and in which new strategies for successful adaptation are being formulated; and (d) 75+, when the individual is concerned with living in a dignified, fulfilled manner, all things being equal.

Obviously, there is some overlap from one period to the next, since there are wide individual differences along a wide range of conditions, such as health and financial status. Doubtless, continuing education has the resources to provide the specific input for a specific aspect of a period depending, to a large extent, on the ingenuity and resources of the adult educator.

Educational Technology

Recent progress in instrumental technology, such as television, radio, film, audiovisual tapes, and computers will not only reduce the cost of instruotion but will also reach large numbers of learners, thereby satisfying some of the needs of life-span education.

Experimental research on the effectiveness of modern technology in adult learning is indeed lacking. However, Lumsden (1975) suggests that the evidence for its effectiveness, as compared to traditional methods of instruction, is equivocal. He reports positive results from the use of programmed materials in the teaching of safety techniques to adults with less than 8 years of formal education. In a study using computer assisted instruction with undereducated adults under varying reinforcement conditions, Lumsden reports that supranormal reinforcement (i.e., reinforcement beyond the knowledge of results) is not related to significant increases in the amount learned.

In another experiment on the effectiveness of modern technology with adults, he reports on multimodal methods of instruction. Lumsden and associates hypothesized that material presented via the audio and visual modalities would not be as effective as that presented over only the visual mode. Again, undereducated adults served as participants. Results failed to support the hypothesis, since the difference in performance did not reach statistical significance. Lumsden interprets these findings, along with the results on computer assisted instruction, to mean that, until further research has been conducted, the benefits in learning derived from these devices cannot be said to justify their enormous cost. Lumsden aptly points out that the limits of automated kinds of instruction are simply unknown.

Although it has been established, to some extent, that programmed forms of instruction lead to the learning of facts, technical terminology, and other relatively simple materials, whether or not these forms lead to the learning of conceptual or other complex cognitive skills has not been established (Lumsden, 1975). Of course, the real question relates to the broad role of adult education. If, on the one hand, its major intent is to help the older learner adapt under survival contingencies, then some form of programmed learning would appear more than adequate. If, on the other hand, the major intent is to focus on the older learners' feelings of worth through philosophical analysis, then some form of multifaceted human interaction, not provided by even the most sophisticated technology, is requisite. It takes more than an adult education unit to deliver both. Obviously, I am referring to the older learner, not the younger adult of recent post high school years who is attending adult education classes to earn a degree.

Winn, Elias, and Marshall (1976) point out that teaching machines require rapid alternation (as in the anticipation method) between storage and retrieval processes in memory, which is less efficient than the study–test method. In addition, these investigators suggest that, since older learners need to process more of a stimulus in order to derive sufficient meaning and are subject to interference from competing associations, programs should emphasize overlearning of concepts while at the same time underscoring differences prior to similarities.

Whatever the form, we have seen from previous chapters that older learners in general need assistance in organizing information for learning and recall. One successful method to accomplish this is through instructions on how to organize material. In addition, I discussed the role of mediators and mnemonic devices (not often used by the older learner) in forming associations or links between informational materials, leading to performance increments. Again, instructions on how to form mental pictures or images is most effective.

In view of the sensory problems concomitant with aging, learning materials should be presented in bold type, programmed material should have increased redundancy, and computer assisted instruction should be geared to the slower response rate of the elderly.

I should like to make some additional suggestions for enhancing the learning performance of older adults, all of which are derived from the research findings discussed throughout the book:

1. Design learning conditions which incorporate the use of the elderly's long history of experience, so that novel material can be related to old to result in organization, leading in turn to better understanding.
2. Proceed from simple tasks, or those that are otherwise familiar, to more complex tasks, always allowing sufficient time for older learners to process input and emit output. (In this connection, the pacing of tasks should be related to reaction time.) Allow self-pacing for best performance.
3. Arrange conditions so that attention is focused and maintained on a single, well-defined bit of information, in view of the increased susceptibility with age to distraction by irrelevant activities and material.
4. Emphasize learning tasks that require abilities which are more resistant to decline, such as verbal abilities, and de-emphasize tasks that require highly abstract processing (unless of course the program includes specific training in the use of higher order skills).
5. Stimulus materials should have distinguishing characteristics (e.g., bold type, large print) to help the older adult to discriminate between stimuli that are similar.
6. Finally, as suggested by Gournard and Hulicka (1977), a light atmosphere, or even one approaching levity, should be maintained in order to reduce tension, the benefits of the reduction of which are clear.

Life-Span Education

Rapidly changing cultural contingencies (including technological advances), increased survival rates, and increased leisure time represent the bases upon which the need for lifelong learning rests. The basic principle here is that education should be construed as a process beginning at an early age and continuing throughout one's life. This concept goes beyond informal education, where one profits from experience and "living," to incorporate formalized, structured programs carried on in an academic manner but not necessarily in a school setting and designed specifically to meet the needs and interests of particular groups of people.

Intellectual development is conceptualized as lying along a continuum, all parts of which, at any given time, are inextricably linked. The proponents of this concept view learning as occurring in other places besides a school classroom, such as libraries, museums, and other similar agencies. The emphasis is placed on total growth through a wide variety of media such as peer groups, family, and a range of contact groups, all of whom are involved in the environmental contingencies which are interacting to shape the individual. In short, a major assumption under which the concept operates is that one's intellectual skills are potentially functional over a lifetime and not simply restricted to the early formal schooling years.

Moreover, rapid change characterizes the current (and projected) human condition, which demands some sort of educational structure to aid people of all ages in an extraordinarily complex adaptation process. Thus, a major purpose of life-span education is to increase the probability of successful adaptation by providing the resources necessary for the retooling of both intellectual and coping skills through the process of learning.

Cropley (1976) reports that a curriculum for the older learner should include opportunities for one to indulge one's curiosity and to have the opportunity to be creative. In addition, the evaluation of one's output should be relative to progress from a specific starting point and not to some arbitrary absolute standard relative to other performance groups. A wide range of individual differences in talent would then be recognized. Along similar lines, Schaie (1974) suggests that "Head Start" kinds of programs should be initiated for the older learner so that they could become more aware of what is happening around them or otherwise have the opportunity to upgrade employment and sociocultural skills. Schaie would have a compulsory education structure similar to that of the early years; however, he would prefer a system of voluntary attendance (which would be sustained through adequate reward contingencies).

Birren and Woodruff (1973) submit a comprehensive proposal for educational intervention throughout the life-span designed particularly for the older learner over 65 but not excluding the younger (aged 45) adult. They submit that, since adults are getting more education through the years, they will likely sustain a marked interest in continued learning beyond the leisure-type course. They point out that new instructional devices and programs will demand a definitive coalition between psychologists and educators, who should design and implement teaching–learning strategies around the interests of learners in lieu of specific age groups.

Since the role of women is changing for a variety of reasons, one of which is that their educational level is increasing substantially, which modifies their role from that of a homemaker to a more visible contributor to society, educational programs will be required to meet their additional needs for expression. In short, education should take the major initiative in constructing environments through which people are helped with developmental tasks throughout the span of life.

Intervention

Intervention strategies of a programmed nature have change as the focal point, whether it is change for the purpose of alleviation or prevention of behavioral deficits or for the enrichment of existing repertoires. Recently, a number of investigators have eschewed the descriptive approach to aging phenomena in favor of a more definitive, behavioral approach, both in the conceptualization of the aging process and in the modification, through the manipulation of environmental contingencies, of presumed age related behaviors (Baltes, 1973). Our interest is with education as a general intervention approach which includes a range of particular strategies, such as operant conditioning for one, designed not only to modify cognitive deficiencies but also, and perhaps more importantly, to prevent potential deficits and to enrich one's current storehouse of experience. One should recognize, of course, that there is ever present the ethical (i.e., means versus ends) issue of behavior modification, since these phenomena are decided upon by groups (controllers) who are defined by idiosyncratic value systems. Historically, we have placed a high value on cognitive functions, and therefore one can easily justify the modification through intervention of any one of a number of specific skills subsumed under "cognition."

The question arises, however, as to whether other target behaviors, such as compassion or general happiness, might be emphasized in addition (Looft, 1973). Looft suggests that energy should be channeled into the affective domain (with an emphasis on prevention of the hopeless–helpless syndrome) in order to select target behavior for modification through, for example, educational curricula.

Looft would have an age integrated society in which people would not be categorized according to age, race, or social class, but would instead be characterized by seemingly diverse value systems and expectations. He argues that the negative effects of our age stratification culture are more pronounced among the aged and that therefore intervention programs should attempt to neutralize the barriers between age cohorts. A specific plan would be to move the elderly back into a home setting environment where they would interact with family members of varied ages or with a family surrogate. The point of this strategy is somewhat obvious, in that an institution is relatively devoid of the kind of stimulation required to maintain cognitive and affective functions at or near their capacity. For those who cannot return to a home setting, the institutional environment should be arranged so that all ages interact in order that the many benefits, the "sense of community," for example, would be realized by an otherwise socially isolated group (Looft, 1973).

A striking irony is that our present educational system is structured so that step by step, year by year, one's cognitive behavior is shaped to approximate that of the adult. Yet the predicament found in our system of higher education in recent times bespeaks of the inadequacy of that age related, hierarchal model, as Looft (1973) aptly points out. In its place he would have lifelong education that provided affective and intellectual rewards, integrated for content and age, so that the goal of becoming a "competitive, achieving adult" would be virtually eliminated.

Looft would have life-span education centers in which young and old would interact to their mutual benefit. Additional target persons would be the "opinion makers and governors of society" (Looft, 1973), who range in age from the middle 40s to the middle 60s and who shape the values and opinions of the culture (Kalish, 1969). The end would be to maximize individual potential, with all of the implications for expression of diverse talents and interests.

Andragogy

Andragogy is taken to mean the art and science of helping the older person learn, as contrasted to pedagogy, the art and science of teaching children (Meyer, 1977). Again, it would appear useful to make such distinctions while at the same time bearing in mind the relationship between the effects emanating from both processes, since they lie along a continuum.

Meyer (1977) published a comparative analysis of the two processes, summarized as follows:

Pedagogy assumes a captive audience composed of young, dependent learners who are there to receive knowledge, the content of which has been arbitrarily decided upon by a teacher mainly concerned with preparing them for the future. What is important is that the learner absorb a body of knowledge so that additional, more complex content can be learned, with little regard to how the individual learner feels about what is being taught. The teacher is defined as an authority more or less beyond question, so that input into the learning process is virtually unidimensional.

Andragogy, on the other hand, assumes that initially the interest of the adult learner must be stimulated before participation in coursework becomes a reality. In this process, the adult learner is viewed as entering any course with a wide background of prior learning and experience which can be utilized for mutual input to define a condition in which the teacher is basically a guide who also benefits from the older learner's input. The learner has input both in the content and in how it will be taught, so that this active involvement leads not only to an enhanced self-concept but also to an increase of knowledge, both consequences leading to the mutual betterment of the participants. Problem solving and principles are important, and one's feeling about course content is viewed as the basis for retention.

In short, pedagogy assumes that a student is moving through the process of learning phenomena toward maturation, at which point andragogy enters the picture and assumes that the learner has already arrived. Andragogy is based on assumptions that older learners are more concerned with solutions or approaches to immediate, rather than to long range, problems; they enter a learning experience with wide, diversified histories, thereby having a particular set to learn; and they are, in general, independent and self-directed.

Meyer (1977) reports that the T-group model provides a viable delivery strategy for the andragogical approach to adult learning. Some of the advantages are that the adult many times feels less anxious when working with a cohort group sharing similar interests; the older learners mutually share a variety of experiences; and traditional lectures, which are oftentimes boring, are supplemented by student participation in learning. For example, courses in preretirement training have used this model in which groups of adults interact (in an educational setting) to provide mutual exchange of information, experience, and feelings. The results have been entirely favorable in that participants have been observed to grow emotionally and intellectually.

Self-Education

That education throughout one's lifetime has become prerequisite to adaptation beyond minimal levels has been amply demonstrated. The problem now is to implement the goals of education on behalf of the individual (and ultimately, of the culture). We have discussed various strategies designed to effect the maximization of potential. Cohen (1977) suggests self-education, not so much as an alternative approach, but as the sine qua non of any educational system in this century of information boom and rapid obsolescence. She submits that change must come in an age graded system where the older teach the younger only to be replaced by a younger counterpart, despite the unused potential of the older. Cohen argues for an educational community in which there is a reciprocal relationship between teacher and learner and in which such roles can be exchanged on a volitional basis.

She would have a self-learning milieu, where individual differences are han-

dled through individualized instruction and where emphasis is placed on inter-
changes between young and old. The goals of education would pivot on individualized learning environments that could meet the demands of a diversity of
talents among a teaching–learning population, since our present linear education
plan is apparently inadequate.

Perceptual-Humanistic Aspects

Wass and West (1977) report that the perceptual (phenomenological) theory
of Combs and Snygg (1959) has direct application to educational programs for
older learners. This theory posits that essentially all behavior is a function of
one's perceptual field, which includes attitudes, needs, and perceptions of experience. The dynamic mechanism, upon which the model pivots, is a "self" that is
defined by idiosyncratic characteristics. Also, the theory encompasses principles
similar to those of humanistic psychology. Wass and West (1977) submit that
education for the older learner should provide for individual differences (one's
uniqueness) within a humanistic context. Thus, they suggest the perceptual-
humanistic approach to educational programming for older adults, and, although
they are in agreement with the traditionalists in stating that learning is central to
any approach, this humanistic variant is advanced as an alternative to the behavioristic model, since it purports to go beyond the learning variables to include recognition of the personal meanings associated with experiencing events.

In short, educational programs generated from within the perceptual–humanistic frame of reference would be characterized by the following guidelines (in
summary form): (*a*) Emphasis would be on the meaning (rather than the behavior) derived from subjective experiences, which are interpreted through internal
mechanisms and which in turn are expressed as feelings, attitudes, and beliefs;
(*b*) Individual learners would have the responsibility of discovering personal
meaning through self-directed effort; (*c*) The concept of self would be defined as
having worth; and, finally, (*d*) Programs would satisfy the needs of a wide variety
of clientele complemented by a range of experiential backgrounds; that is, these
programs would be flexible and personalized.

Value Tendencies

Earlier we discussed the study conducted by March, Hooper, and Baum (1977)
in which they found less than positive interest on the part of elderly persons in
participating in formal educational programs. These groups equated living with
learning.

Not unrelated is a study conducted by Daniel, Templin, and Shearon (1977)
to determine value orientations toward education. They administered a questionnaire to 10,000+ community college students, 311 of whom were aged 60 or
over. Participants were asked to specify their reasons for continuing their education. The results indicate that the aged 60+ respondents are oriented toward

sociocultural and improvement learning dimensions; for example, to make a contribution to society and to learn new things, respectively.

Although this study tells us what apparently motivated these older persons to continue their education, the conclusions are generalizable only to those persons attending and not to the majority of elderly persons, who are not attending. At any rate, the investigators urge educators of adults to recognize such factors in attendance and to design appropriate programs, since the programs available and their physical setting are significant variables in attracting older learners.

Creativity

Creativity is usually defined as a cognitive process out of which one produces a work that is novel or significant or both, and which is otherwise judged to be a marked contribution to a particular segment of the culture or to the whole of society itself. The notion involves the discovery of something original or the elucidation of some unsolved problem, such as the breaking down of the DNA/RNA code. As an intellectual process, we are faced again with the problem of how it is measured and what the qualitative and quantitative criteria are. Similar to the study of intelligence, the stability of creativity is related to one's definition of the concept.

Kogan (1973) suggests three approaches (sometimes also referred to as "divergent thinking" [Guilford, 1967] approaches) to the study of creativity. One is seen to take a different, new approach to solving a problem or answering a query through emphasis either on the product, the personality, or the process. It would appear more useful for our purposes to limit our discussion to the product approach and to the role of the educators of adults in encouraging creative output and achievement over the life-span.

An early study of Lehman (1953) indicated that chemists and mathematicians reached their peak in creative contributions between the ages of 25 and 30, whereas the quality of contributions peaked out for philosophers between the ages of 35 and 40 and for authors before age 45. A general conclusion was that creativity peaks in the thirties and gradually declines over the life-span and that the quality of contributions declined earlier than the quantity. In later studies Lehman (1962, 1966) suggests that the observed decline was not a function of intellectual degeneration but rather was more closely related to societal role expectations and attitudes. More importantly, he interpreted the results to indicate that wide individual differences in the literature and the science areas demonstrate that creative potential is not restricted by age itself.

Dennis (1956, 1966) suggested that the Lehman studies were limited for a variety of reasons, the major one being that they compared contributions of men of different longevity, thereby biasing the results; that is, work completed by some people before their early deaths was compared with that of people who had longer working periods in which to make contributions.

Dennis (1966) conducted a study of the creative contributions of long-lived persons and reported results contrary to those of Lehman. He found peaks in productivity throughout the later years. His study was based on quantity rather than on quality as were the Lehman studies, which may account for the differences between their results; however, it would appear that there is the additional confounding factor of judging what is meant by "quality," despite the fact that objectivity and subjectivity enter into both quantity and quality observations.

In any case, it would behoove the educator of adults to conceptualize creativity as having no age limit and as to be expected in some form throughout the later years. In order to foster creativity in the classroom, Stein (1974) would have teachers and administrative staff members working together in the planning and implementation both of course content and of delivery method, thus assuming that older people can learn new things and can approach problems in new ways if given the encouragement and the opportunity. Creative adult education would include a wide range of courses in aesthetics and art in order to meet the varying needs of a wide range of individuals. Content would have an emphasis on divergent ways to solve problems, on new forms of literature, and on different cultures.

The delivery model for creative kinds of output would include an environment in which divergent thinking and expression under relative non-failure conditions is encouraged, in lieu of the convergent (one correct answer) type. A problem here, of course, is that the present generation of older teachers were trained under convergent conditions and would therefore require some form of encouragement to try new approaches to the teaching–learning process (Alpaugh, Renner, & Birren, 1976). Focus would be on novelty of response for certain materials rather than on its "correctness" or usability, which could be effected through teacher instructions.

As Alpaugh *et al.* (1976) point out, although definitive information is lacking about the creative process itself, educators can stimulate it in older learners and, indeed, have the responsibility to encourage "novel manipulations of previously learned material and different ways of perceiving the environment [p. 37]."

NEEDS AND INTERESTS

Earlier I indicated that although opportunities for continuing one's education are present, the elderly are observed as not participating, to a large extent, in the programs offered, for a variety of reasons (Wasserman, 1976; Webber, 1963). It would appear that motivation to develop further is somewhat lacking. Webber (1963) suggests that lack of participation in continuing education activities could be a function of society's role expectations, since the elderly have most restricted roles in a capitalistic, technologically oriented system. In addition, the ostensible lack of participation and interest could be related to their needs not having been satisfied, since the physical settings, etc. are more often than not inadequate.

Developmental factors

Wasserman (1976) reports low interest among the elderly aged 65 and over in adult education; however, the interest level of persons aged 55–64 was relatively high, and therefore he suggests that future planning, in preretirement training, for example, should be directed towards this age group. Arling (1977) points out a sampling bias in Wasserman's study, since low socioeconomic status subjects were used. Arling argues that persons of higher income and better educational background tend to avail themselves more of educational opportunities than do persons of lower status. More importantly, perhaps, Wasserman suggested that the results were a function of chronological age but fails to point out that other factors such as health and educational level also influence interest (Arling, 1977).

Havighurst (1972) submits that learning is essential over the life-span in order to satisfy needs that fluctuate with specific, changing developmental tasks and that these needs should be met through the medium of continuing education, which he describes as consisting of instrumental and expressive components (Havighurst, 1976). Instrumental learning refers to those activities through which one learns to adapt to changing conditions or otherwise learns some new skill instrumental in some sort of achievement. Expressive learning refers to activities leading to personal life satisfaction and self-expression. As indicated earlier, the aspects are complementary.

Hiemstra (1976) conducted a study to determine adult interest in these two types of learning and found that subjects aged 55 and over express significant preference for instrumental learning as opposed to expressive, both in course choices and in actual learning projects. In addition, this group displays a relatively wide range of educational interests and have been involved in learning activities on a consistent basis. The author suggests that the educators of adults should emphasize instrumental learning activities in programming, while at the same time making the programs available and attractive so as to encourage actual participation.

In another study, Hiemstra (1976) found that subjects aged 55 and over and of a higher socioeconomic and educational status were involved, to a significant degree, in more learning projects than subjects in a lower status group. However, the "blue collar workers" in this study were engaged in a significant number of hours of learning activity, which is interpreted as attenuating some of the stereotype about the educational interests of particular minority groups.

Graney and Hays (1976) report that in a study of subjects aged 62+ relatively high interest as compared to the earlier studies in higher education was expressed. A significant amount of interest by a large minority of people was expressed in courses in the liberal arts and in science and nature, followed by interest in arts and crafts kinds of activities. His results are consistent with other findings that posit that interest is related to prior educational achievement. For the large minority of persons interested in taking college classes, the authors report that the most important barriers were information and costs and, for disinterested subjects, negative attitudes toward themselves.

Information Lag

In a general way, I have discussed the rapid obsolescence of knowledge concomitant with a rapidly changing society. More specifically, and for example, Dubin (1972, 1974) reports that within five years after completion of a degree program in engineering, engineers will need further education to compensate for the virtual obsolescence of what they had learned. McGlynn (1976) points out that what one knows about engineering now will be reduced 50% in ten years in the absence of continuing education, either through course work or research. For the basic sciences, 50% obsolescence is predicted within seven years.

The implications of this condition are enormously complicated, since more than taking courses within an adult or continuing education framework is involved. In order to alleviate the effects of this situation (generalizable to sectors other than that of engineering), there are a range of psychological variables, such as sense of competence and motivation to continue to learn after one's full-time formal education has been completed, which must be considered (Arvey & Neel, 1976). Dubin charges education with the responsibility of encouraging personal initiative for the sustained involvement of older learners in their adaptive functions, so that mutual needs are satisfied.

Death and Dying

There has been a recent spate of interest in the subject of death and dying, as is found in the increasing number of institutions that are offering formal courses at all levels, from within a range of academic disciplines, and to a variety of clientele. Apparently, there has been a general change of attitude toward discussion of this once taboo topic; however, some question remains as to whether or not the attitude of those for whom death is most imminent (i.e., the aged) is being reciprocally affected by what is happening in the universities, the high schools, and the media, all of which is marked by openness and candidness on death and dying. Wass (1977), therefore, designed a study in which 171 volunteer subjects aged 65+ responded to a 23 item survey questionnaire dealing with virtually every aspect of the death and dying phenomenon. She then performed a comparative analysis of her data with that derived from a similar questionnaire given to a significantly younger group by Schneidman (1971), who reported an N of 30,000 (which is in itself instructive, since it underscores a need to talk about death).

Results indicate that a significantly higher percentage of the elderly view death as a new beginning, as contrasted to the younger group, who construe death as the end. The older group were more concerned with the pain potentially concomitant with dying and the grief it would effect in their loved ones than was the Schneidman group. When asked how often death enters their thoughts, 22.2% of the aged responded "never," which is curious indeed. Equally interesting is the fact that 60.4% expressed pleasure in being alive when they do experience thoughts of death, and only 1.7% stated they feared death when they thought of their own. In short, there were significant differences in the beliefs toward an afterlife and toward last rites, the elderly being more disposed to an earth burial with accompanying rituals.

Wass interprets the data from this study as indicative of the need for continuing (adult) education to neutralize the reluctance of the general public to talk freely with the aged themselves about death. So that the wishes of the elderly concerning their own death and burial are consistent with the attitudes of those who will deal with the situation (namely, funeral directors), adult educators should plan courses or programs to bridge the gaps that exist here. A significant majority of the aged want to be informed of any terminal illness and wish to die a natural death, the implications of which for education are clear, since this kind of information needs to be disseminated.

The topical area of death and dying can be delivered through the same variety of presentation procedures as any other subject matter; however, Kurlychek (1977) points out that, regardless of the technique, "the inescapable fact is that attention to death as a subject matter ultimately confronts the individual with some dimension of personal death [p. 44]." Death education can be defined as a process through which one perceives death as a reality to be integrated into the total life cycle (Kurlychek, 1977), as one of a number of organizing principles (Feifel, 1959), and as a highly constructive dimension of life (Kubler-Ross, 1975).

Death education has a number of purposes beyond the philosophical, one of which is to better prepare individuals for the dying phenomenon, while at the same time modifying the degree of fear of death but not eliminating it entirely, since some fear is certainly adaptive, the results of which are related to the ultimate betterment of the culture. Research as to the effectiveness of death education programs is sparse, not only because of its recency, but also because of methodological limitations related to the lack of control groups; therefore, any conclusions at this point would appear premature.

ATTITUDES

That strong negative stereotypes of the aged are widely held across age levels has been well documented in the research literature (Kogan, 1961; Peterson & Peters, 1971; Tuckman & Lorge, 1953). However, Harris and Associates (1975) published the results of an exhaustive poll taken from a wide range of groups and ages which attentuates the validity of such attitudes.

In summary form, he and his associates found:

1. The majority of older people in the United States wish to continue contributing to society and to work up to their potential.
2. The old themselves have negative attitudes toward aging and the aged. A substantial number of old people stated that their life is better after age 65 than before, but they felt that they were the exception, since most older people are in poor conditions, both fiscally and intellectually.
3. The general public felt strongly that poor health was a major problem for the elderly, whereas a substantial number of older people themselves felt not so strongly about it.
4. Crises classed as "very serious" are similar for those aged 18–64 years and for those aged 65+, with the exception of health problems and of the potential to be a victim of crime. In short, persons aged 65+ were in agreement with those younger than 65 that most people over 65 have problems as just summarized, but individual respondents over age 65 viewed themselves as the exception.
5. The public views people over 65 as leading isolated, sedentary lives, but this poll indicates that older persons engage in a wide range of activities, to a considerable extent.
6. The majority of older people prefer to become involved in age-integrated activities.
7. A minority of younger persons view older people as productive, contributing members of society, whereas the older persons view themselves as most useful in their community.
8. Approximately five million persons aged 65+ volunteer their services to various sectors of society, and an additional substantial number have expressed interest in making themselves available for service.

The findings in the literature concerning the attitudes of young adults and adolescents toward the elderly are equivocal (Ivester & King, 1977), and the mechanisms involved in the formation of attitudes are a critical area of research in educational gerontology (Ansello, 1977). That the notion of attitude, defined as a stable and lasting predisposition to act in a specific way towards persons, objects, or events, is central in social psychology (to which gerontology most certainly is linked) has been underscored by Allport (1968). Ivester and King (1977) conducted a study in which 439 students with a mean age of fifteen served as subjects. Results indicate that the majority of adolescents expressed a positive attitude toward old people. Attitude was observed to vary with class and race, the middle class showing a more positive attitude than the lower class and whites showing more than non-whites. The authors suggest that since the earlier studies in the 1950s and 1960s people in general have come to more readily accept the elderly, possibly because of more education and because of exposure through the media to the conditions of the aged. They urge further study on the nature of contact, since the data of this study indicate that frequency of contact is not directly related to attitudes toward the elderly, which would appear somewhat at variance with the notions of Festinger (1964), who suggests that congruency of attitudes is a function of the extent of exposure between subject–subject or subject–object. This assumption may not be valid when applied to the aged, since the total context in which they are exposed may be partially negative by nature. In any case, the ambiguities here need to be resolved.

Literature and Students

Jencks (1972) and Peterson (1975) suggested that prior to one's entrance into formal schooling, one will have learned a variety of attitudes and values toward a range of people and things, which will in turn be highly resistant to change or modification. Ansello (1977) conducted a comprehensive review of children's first literature and reports that the older person is usually depicted as being "relatively unimportant, unexciting, and unimaginative [p. 269]" as opposed to being articulate and otherwise independent, thus leading to a stereotype of someone less than exciting and creative. The impact of literature is suggested as a powerful factor in the formation of attitudes toward the aged (which may or may not be amenable to modification through intervention strategies, such as education).

Peterson and Eden (1977) reported the results of a content analysis of adolescent literature which was conducted in order to determine the picture portrayed of the older person. Results indicate that although the older person was visible in most of the books, he/she was not developed as a main character, which suggests that they were assigned something less than a major role in the work. These findings are consistent with those of Ansello (1977) in that the older person is depicted as being somewhat boring and relatively unimportant. Adolescent literature is observed to emphasize the youth culture with its theme of beauty and vigor. These authors suggest that the literature should portray the older person in more complex and in patently positive ways.

From another perspective, Schaie (1973) suggests that intervention strategies focus on the young and middle aged in an effort to neutralize the effects of an age-graded society, which he views as directly related to current views of aging. Perhaps the literature should reflect scenarios of age-integrated interactions in which young and old are functioning in reciprocal roles characterized by alternating expectations.

Ideally, substantive changes in the current literature of school age children in their formative years would be forthcoming. From a practical standpoint, the enormous administrative complexities involved in curricular modification (which are preceded by the process of clarification of the ambiguities of the mechanisms used in attitude formation) indicate that changes on a grand scale would be gradual. Another alternative among many to be used in breaking down stereotypes would be to offer courses in gerontology. Seltzer (1977) reports that students completing coursework which stressed the positive or otherwise normal aspects of aging expressed a more positive attitude toward the aged than the one they previously held. As part of the course, students worked in the field with the aged, which was described as a highly significant experience leading to attitude change. In addition, students stated that they were now better equipped to adapt to their own eventual aging process. Seltzer points out that the transmission of the information about the aged may not be as important as the teacher's own behavior toward aging phenomena.

Gordon and Hallauer (1976) investigated the effects of a course involving both field and class work on attitudes toward the aged. They report that a course in aging is related significantly to changes in the attitudes of college-aged students. Moreover, the "friendly visit" aspect (notwithstanding transportation exigencies) had a greater impact in modifying the attitudes both of the aged and of the students.

HIGHER EDUCATION

Recently, an upsurge in interest has been observed for long-range funding of the education of the aged through such federal bureaucratic structures as the National Institute of Mental Health, the Administration on Aging, and the Office of Education, to name a few. Since institutions of higher learning are directly or indirectly involved in the bulk of research and development concerning aging and since they have the resources (e.g., delivery systems) to interpret and disseminate information derived from their studies, some investigators have charged them with the responsibility to take the major initiative in continuing education and in lifelong learning programs.

Role of Higher Education

Erlich and Erlich (1976) report a four-part frame of reference out of which most institutions of higher learning could operate both to meet their responsibilities to society in general and to meet the needs of an aging population in particular.

In summary form, this four-part model suggests the following for institutions of higher education:

1. They should provide learning environments (e.g., new curricula) in which persons who are middle-aged or older can begin new careers or otherwise broaden their cultural and educational base so that they can continue making contributions to society, which in turn satisfies mutual needs. Such environments would include the opening of doors to the older learner to participate in age-integrated classes or any other alternative combinations of teacher–student relationships.

2. They should provide education about the phenomena of aging to all learners throughout the educational system so that both one's attitude toward the aged and aging and one's adaptive strategies could be favorably affected.

3. They should provide continuing education and training for service personnel, both to increase their effectiveness and to encourage, through interdisciplinary courses and such devices as workshops on the needs of the elderly, new workers to enter the field.

4. They should take the initiative in research and development and should disseminate new findings through, for example, demonstration, to the service systems. Research and implementation would involve researchers (who could be retired scientists, for example) and service practitioners working together in a total cooperative effort within or outside the university system.

That the number of persons who participate in continuing education programs is increasing (Havighurst, 1976) and that they learn as well and sometimes better than they did in the past (Blau, 1973) is being recognized by the public in general and by the political sector in particular. Mondale (1975), at that time a senator, proposed a lifelong-learning bill which would provide a wide range of alternatives for the older learner who would participate in an educational program. Lifelong learning is defined as programs designed to modify the knowledge, skills, and attitudes of people who are no longer enrolled in the traditional school system. The Commissioner of Education was charged with the co-ordination of federal support and with suggesting alternative ways to finance life-span education. Provisions were made for state agencies to assess existing programs, to provide for the training of service practitioners, and to develop curricula and an entire delivery system model. Recommendations to the White House were to be made by January 1, 1978. The passing of a bill with such comprehensive dimensions would have a wide range of economic, social, and psychological effects. In short, existing physical plants that are not being fully utilized could be used by older learners, to mutual benefit.

Undergraduate Training in Aging

I have already discussed a number of compelling reasons for the study of aging. Hulicka and Morganti (1976) strongly urge the expansion of gerontological education at all levels and provide a description of a program in this area, operating out of an undergraduate psychology department within a liberal arts context. The goals of their program, in summary, are to make available a range of specialized courses designed to meet a wide variety of individual needs while at the same time arousing interest in the study of aging; to be instrumental in the modification of attitudes toward aging and the aged, and to provide participants who complete the program's requirements with the credentials either to begin advanced work or to enter the field of gerontology at service levels. These observers suggest that education in gerontology is a social obligation which, if implemented in new and broader directions, would benefit the field in particular and the culture in general.

A number of institutions have already implemented structured programs designed essentially for the training of graduate students in gerontology. Undergraduate programs typically qualify one to enter the field as a semiprofessional or in service personnel. However, new and additional programs are sparse, and part of the responsibility to resolve this situation falls on the professor, who should arouse interest in the topical area as an inducement for students to enter careers in gerontology and should articulate the relationship of the issues involved in aging to other academic disciplines. Whitbourne (1977) suggests that educators should identify the goals of their students and should incorporate the gerontological perspective within a course in order to meet the specific needs or goals of those enrolled, so that, regardless of long-range goals, the study of aging would be related to them either directly or in a tangential sense, but in any case would broaden the frame of reference of the enrollee. Obviously, the goals and interests of the full-time undergraduate student would differ from those of the continuing education student, who is typically older and already gainfully employed in a position or career.

Whitbourne (1977) suggests that the goals of both the instructor and the student can be realized through substantive course offerings presented through lectures or seminars and augmented by some sort of field work or physical contact with the elderly themselves, which can be effected through "friendly visiting," a research project in which the elderly serves as subjects, or through community service, in which students would work in a local agency dealing with aging.

Schonfield and Chatfield (1976) delineate the purposes of an undergraduate course, "Introduction to Gerontology," which in the main has the common aims shared by most other introductory courses in the social, behavioral, and natural sciences that are offered within a liberal arts context—namely, to help students think and write clearly, to review major research studies while at the same time gaining an understanding of the nature of research design in gerontology through, for example, personal encounter with the aged, and to relate the problems of aging and the research data to real life situations, all of which has a liberalizing effect on the participants.

As stated earlier, the field of gerontology involves, at the very minimum, the disciplines of biology, sociology, and psychology. Therefore, even at the introductory level, courses in aging should probably have a prerequisite of a principles course in any of the disciplines mentioned. These investigators suggest that at present gerontology should be a speciality area within an academic department, such as psychology, until such time as the field becomes coherent or otherwise represents a unified position.

New Directions

Knowlton (1977) reports on the work of a network of institutions of higher learning that provide, on campus, college level coursework of a short term nature for the older learner, called "Elderhostel." Most of the participants live in college dormitories and engage in the typical activities of a full-time student, including taking courses from the regular faculty. The "Elderhostel" plan assumes that a major problem in the aging process is found in the stereotype, held by both the elderly themselves and the general public, of the older person as dependent and otherwise non-productive. One strategy to neutralize the effects of this condition (and ultimately to prevent recurrence) is to get them onto a campus and involved in its excitement and its atmosphere of intellectual stimulation. Knowlton reports that since its inception in 1975 the program has been judged by participants and educators as highly successful. The author reports that this plan is viewed as a more attractive form of continuing education, since it: (a) provides an opportunity for a brief change of environment characterized by a refreshing kind of excitement; (b) provides a compacted time span more functional than attending class one period per week over several months; and (c) provides regular college courses at relatively low cost, as opposed to courses especially designed for the elderly. Knowlton points out that the courses offered met the standards of the typical college course offering, with an emphasis on courses in the liberal arts tradition.

Some researchers suggest that a substantial number of older persons should be encouraged to either begin new careers or take up another career so that both society and the individual can benefit through the utilization of their residual potential, which usually dissipates at or near retirement. Sheppard (1976) submits that a vehicle to handle that situation is career education designed mainly for the training or retraining of older persons to work in positions of service to others. He views career education as encompassing vocational education specifically directed at increasing the older person's interest in continued working, so that they would take the necessary training in skill development to once again become productive members of society.

The mass media has taken on a significant role in terms of the varied opportunities it provides for learning in a non-classroom setting, such as college level courses by newspaper (Lewis, 1974). A substantial number of colleges and universities are offering credit courses taught by distinguished faculty via the newspaper. Among several obvious advantages to this modality is the fact that virtually all learners have the opportunity to learn in a relatively nonthreatening environment, although evaluation is part of the course requirement, along with two contact sessions, one at midterm and one at the end of the course.

SUMMARY AND FINAL COMMENT

Life-span education refers to the kind of educational structure which operates on assumptions provided by life-span developmental psychologists. It typically involves a planned series of activities in which one can increase a knowledge store and enhance skills. Through this process, one's attitude toward aging and the aged is changed so that the potential for more than adequate adaptation is realized, thereby establishing a better condition for the culture. A variety of public and private institutions are directly involved in the design and implementation of life-span education principles.

Recently the term "lifelong learning" has come into usage in the field of aging. This concept refers to learning in the broadest sense, more or less to that learning of an incidental and informal nature (relative to life-span education) that occurs throughout one's life. Although it focuses on the need for intellectual activity and it may include structured and planned programs, it usually refers to what is learned during the course of life as a function of non-goal (i.e., educational) directed behavior.

Life-span developmental psychologists submit that development is a lifelong process for which education has a key role in that education can assist people in resolving the demands of developmental tasks defined by specific periods across the age continuum. It has been suggested that educational institutions must change to satisfy the needs and interests of people, regardless of age.

The age structure of our culture is changing because of a decline in birth rate and an increase in longevity brought about by medical and technological advances, to the extent that institutions of learning will have an older constituency in the very near future. In addition, a further burden (responsibility) will be placed on our educational institutions, since each succeeding generation is becoming more educated and will predictably demand continued education and training.

Compounding this situation is the fact that technological changes increase information and skill obsolescence rates both for those presently in the work force and for those in retirement. Women have taken on new and additional responsibilities within the social structure. The elderly (and other subcultures) are intellectually deprived. All of these factors taken individually and collectively provide the appropriate agencies with the basis upon which they can take a life-span approach to education.

I have discussed a variety of intervention strategies throughout the book, one of which involves education as a mechanism for change. A major priority is to alleviate educational deprivation, a factor which accounts for a substantial portion of the observed variance in performance parameters. Some investigators suggest that education focus on or shift to affective experience in lieu of cognitive, since the former is more directly related to the adaptive needs of later life.

Age-integrated training and educational settings have been suggested in order to modify negative attitudes and stereotypes held both by the young and by the elderly.

Finally, I am inclined to believe that the operant model provides a highly effective overall intervention strategy that lends itself well to immediate inclusion in educational programming. I have observed its success in changing performance (behavior) in a variety of situations.

Indeed, the time has come to identify both the antecedent and the consequent circumstances of behavior found in the external environment, notwithstanding the ambiguous and otherwise subtle role the environment has in the selection process. Operant behavior (i.e., that which operates to affect circumstances) can be analyzed simply by arranging environmental conditions for which identifiable effects (consequences) are contingent. There is little doubt that the environment can be manipulated to yield relatively rapid, marked results. The assumptions of operant conditioning, of course, make possible the conditions for optimism in an otherwise negative situation for the elderly in general.

REFERENCES

ALLPORT, G. W. The historical background of modern social psychology. In G. Lindzey & E. Aronson (Eds.), *The handbook of social psychology*, Vol. 1. Reading, Mass.: Addison Wesley, 1968.

ALPAUGH, P. K., RENNER, V. J., & BIRREN, J. E. Age and creativity: Implications for education and teachers. *Educational Gerontology: An International Quarterly,* 1976, *1,* 17-40.

ANSELLO, E. F. Age and ageism in children's first literature. *Educational Gerontology: An International Quarterly,* 1977, *2,* 255-274.

ARLING, G. Comment on Wasserman's study. *Educational Gerontology: An International Quarterly,* 1977, *2,* 191-193.

ARVEY, R. D., & NEEL, C. W. Motivation and obsolescence in engineers. *Industrial Gerontology,* 1976, *3,* 113-120.

BALTES, P. B. Strategies for psychological intervention in old age: A symposium. *The Gerontologist,* 1973, *13,* 4-6.

BIRREN, J. E., & WOODRUFF, D. S. Human development over the lifespan through education. In P. B. Baltes & K. W. Schaie (Eds.), *Life span developmental psychology: Personality and socialization.* New York: Academic Press, 1973.

BLAU, Z. S. *Old age in a changing society.* New York: Franklin Watts, 1973.

COHEN, D. An exposition of the concept of lifelong self education. *Educational Gerontology: An International Quarterly,* 1977, *2,* 157-162.

COMBS, A. W., & SNYGG, D. *Individual behavior: A perceptual approach to behavior.* New York: Harper & Row, 1959.

CROPLEY, A. J. Some psychological reflections on lifelong education. In R. H. Dave (Ed.), *Foundations of lifelong education.* UNESCO Institute for Education: Pergamon Press, 1976.

DANIEL, D. E., TEMPLIN, R. G., & SHEARON, R. W. The value orientations of older adults toward education. *Educational Gerontology: An International Quarterly,* 1977, *2,* 33-42.

DENNIS, W. Age and achievement: A critique. *Journal of Gerontology,* 1956, *11,* 331-333.

DENNIS, W. Creative productivity between ages 20 and 80 years. *Journal of Gerontology,* 1966, *21,* 1-8.

DUBIN, S. S. Obsolescence or lifelong education: A choice for the professional. *American Psychologist,* 1972, *27,* 486-498.

DUBIN, S. S. The psychology of lifelong learning. New developments in the professions. *International Review of Applied Psychology,* 1974, *23,* 17-31.

ERLICH, I. F., & ERLICH, P. D. A four part framework to meet the responsibilities of higher education to gerontology. *Educational Gerontology: An International Quarterly,* 1976, *1,* 251-260.

FEIFEL, H. *The meaning of death.* New York: McGraw-Hill, 1959.

FESTINGER, L. Cognitive dissonance. In E. E. Sampson (Ed.), *Approaches, contexts and problems of social psychology.* Englewood Cliffs, N.J.: Prentice-Hall, 1964.

GORDON, S. K., & HALLAUER, D. S. Impact of a friendly visiting program on attitudes of college students toward the aged. *The Gerontologist,* 1976, *16*(4), 371-376.

GOUNARD, B. R., & HULICKA, I. M. Maximizing learning efficiency in later adulthood: A cognitive problem solving approach. *Educational Gerontology: An International Quarterly,* 1977, *2,* 417-427.

GRANEY, M. S., & HAYS, W. C. Senior students: Higher education after age 62. *Educational Gerontology: An International Quarterly,* 1976, *1,* 343-359.

GUILFORD, J. P. *The nature of human intelligence.* New York: McGraw-Hill, 1967.

HARRIS, L., & ASSOCIATES, *The myth and reality of aging in America.* Washington, D.C.: The National Council on Aging, 1975.

HAVIGHURST, R. J. *Developmental tasks and education.* New York: McKay, 1972, Third edition.

HAVIGHURST, R. J. Education through the adult life span. *Educational Gerontology: An International Quarterly,* 1976, *1,* 41–51.

HIEMSTRA, R. Older adult learning: Instrumental and expressive categories. *Educational Gerontology: An International Quarterly,* 1976, *1,* 227–236.

HIEMSTRA, R. The older adult's learning projects. *Educational Gerontology: An International Quarterly,* 1976, *1,* 331–341.

HOULE, C. O. The changing goals of education in the perspective of lifelong learning. *International Review of Education,* 1974, *20,* 430–446.

HULICKA, I. M., & MORGANTI, J. B. An undergraduate concentration in the psychology of aging: Approach, program, and evaluation. *Educational Gerontology: An International Quarterly,* 1976, *1,* 107–118.

IVESTER, C., & KING, K. Attitudes of adolescents toward the aged. *The Gerontologist,* 1977, *17*(1), 85–89.

JENCKS, C. *Inequality: A reassessment of the effect of family and schooling in America.* New York: Basic Books, 1972.

KALISH, R. A. The old and the new as generation gap allies. *Gerontologist,* 1969, *9,* 83–89.

KNOWLTON, M. P. Liberal arts: The Elderhostel plan for survival. *Educational Gerontology: An International Quarterly,* 1977, *2,* 87–93.

KOGAN, N. Attitudes toward old people: The development of a scale and examination of correlates. *Journal of Abnormal and Social Psychology,* 1961, *62,* 44–54.

KOGAN, N. Creativity and cognitive style: A lifespan perspective. In P. B. Baltes & K. W. Schaie (Eds.), *Lifespan developmental psychology: Personality and socialization.* New York: Academic Press, 1973.

KUBLER-ROSS, E. *Death: The final stage of growth.* Englewood Cliffs, N.J.: Prentice-Hall, 1975.

KURLYCHEK, R. T. Death education: Some considerations of purpose and rationale. *Educational Gerontology: An International Quarterly,* 1977, *2,* 43–50.

LEHMAN, H. C. *Age and achievement.* Princeton: Princeton University Press, 1953.

LEHMAN, H. C. The creative production rates of present versus past generations of scientists. *Journal of Gerontology,* 1962, *17,* 409–417.

LEHMAN, H. C. The psychologist's most creative years. *American Psychologist,* 1966, *21,* 363–369.

LEWIS, C. A. Courses by newspaper. In D. W. Vermilye (Ed.), *Lifelong learners—A new clientele for higher education.* San Francisco: Jossey-Bass, 1974.

LIVERIGHT, A. A. *Study of adult education in the United States.* Boston: Center for the Study of Liberal Education for Adults, 1968.

LOOFT, W. R. Reflections on intervention in old age: Motives, goals and assumptions. *American Psychologist,* 1973, *13,* 6–10.

LUMSDEN, D. B. Adult learning and the applications of modern educational technology. In D. B. Lumsden & R. H. Sherron (Eds.), *Experimental studies in adult learning and memory.* Washington, D.C.: Hemisphere, 1975.

MARCH, G. B., HOOPER, J. O., & BAUM, J. Lifespan education and the older adult: Living is learning. *Educational Gerontology: An International Quarterly,* 1977, 2, 163-172.

MCGLYNN, S. P. A few priorities. In *Public forum on financing higher education in Louisiana.* Louisiana State University, 1976.

MEYER, S. L. Andragogy and the aging adult learner. *Educational Gerontology: An International Quarterly,* 1977, 2, 115-122.

MONDALE, W. F. *Congressional Record,* 94th Congress, 1st Session, 10-8-75, p. 17744.

PETERSON, D. A. Life span education and gerontology. *The Gerontologist,* 1975, 436-441.

PETERSON, D. A. The role of gerontology in adult education. In R. A. Kalish (Ed.), *The later years: Social applications of gerontology.* California: Brooks Cole, 1977.

PETERSON, D. A., & EDEN, D. Z. Teenagers and aging: Adolescent literature as an attitude source. *Educational Gerontology: An International Quarterly,* 1977, 2, 311-325.

PETERSON, W. A., & PETERS, G. R. (Eds.), Perceptions of aging. *Gerontologist,* 1971, 11, 59-108.

SCHAIE, K. W. Reflections on papers by Looft, Peterson and Sparks: Intervention toward an ageless society? *The Gerontologist,* 1973, 13, 31-35.

SCHAIE, K. W. Translations in Gerontology— From lab to life. Intellectual functioning. *American Psychologist,* 1974, 802-807.

SCHNEIDMAN, E. S. You and death. *Psychology Today,* 1971, 43-45.

SCHONFIELD, D. Translations in gerontology—From lab to life. Utilizing information. *American Psychologist,* 1974, 796-801.

SCHONFIELD, D., & CHATFIELD, S. Goals, purposes, and future of undergraduate education in the psychology of aging. *Educational Gerontology: An International Quarterly,* 1976, 1, 391-397.

SELTZER, M. M. Differential impact of various experiences on breaking down age stereotypes. *Educational Gerontology: An International Quarterly,* 1977, 2, 183-189.

SHEPPARD, N. A. Career education for older people. *Educational Gerontology: An International Quarterly,* 1976, 1, 399-412.

STEIN, M. I. *Stimulating creativity (Vol. I): Individual procedures.* New York: Academic Press, 1974.

TUCKMAN, J., & LORGE, I. Attitudes toward old people. *Journal of Social Psychology,* 1953, 37, 249-260.

WASS, H. Views and opinions of elderly persons concerning death. *Educational Gerontology: An International Quarterly,* 1977, 2, 15-26.

WASS, H., & WEST, C. A. A humanistic approach to education of older learners. *Educational Gerontology: An International Quarterly,* 1977, 2, 407-416.

WASSERMAN, I. M. The educational interests of the elderly: A case study. *Journal of Educational Gerontology: An International Quarterly,* 1976, 1, 323-330.

WEBBER, I. The educable aged. In J. C. Dixon (Ed.), *Continuing education in the later years.* Gainsville: University of Florida Press, 1963.

WHITBOURNE, S. K. Goals of undergraduate education in gerontology. *Educational Gerontology: An International Quarterly,* 1977, 2, 131-139.

WINN, F. J. JR., ELIAS, J. W., & MARSHALL, P. H. Meaningfulness and interference as factors in paired-associate learning with the aged. *Educational Gerontology: An International Quarterly,* 1976, 1, 297-306.

Subject Index